Let's Think through Science! 8 & 9

Teacher's Guide

Anne Robertson and
Philip Adey

nferNelson
understanding potential

Published by nferNelson Publishing Company Ltd.
The Chiswick Centre
414 Chiswick High Road
London W4 5TF, UK

nferNelson is a division of Granada Learning Limited, part of Granada plc

Designed by Oxford Designers & Illustrators
Printed in the UK by Thanet Press

Code 0090008983 ISBN 0 7087 1439 0 1(9.04)

Contents

Acknowledgements

The schools that trialled *Let's Think through Science! 8 & 9* were all in the London Boroughs of Hammersmith and Fulham, and Harrow. We are extremely grateful for the encouragement and support we have received from these education authorities. Gillian Palmer, Chief Inspector in Hammersmith, has maintained a supportive overview of the project and created the conditions in which the trials could be conducted effectively. Sue Sissling, science inspector in Harrow, has been deeply involved in the implementation of the project, arranging and participating actively in the professional development days, communicating effectively with the headteachers and science teachers from Harrow who have been involved, and generally acting as a 'critical friend' as the project has developed.

The Year 4 teachers and science coordinators in the schools have been enormously supportive and helpful. Their willingness to try out new activities and teaching methods, to be observed and to offer detailed feedback has been invaluable. We owe them a real debt of gratitude, as we do the project school Heads who were willing to risk their Year 4 teachers and pupils experimenting with some quite new ideas, even in an environment of 'high stakes' testing and sometimes unimaginative national inspection systems.

The Year 4 teachers were largely recruited as a result of their schools' participation in *Let's Think through Science!* for seven- and eight-year-olds (Adey *et al.*, 2003), which was partially funded by AstraZeneca. We are grateful to AstraZeneca for its support.

About the Authors

Philip Adey and Anne Robertson also authored the hugely successful programmes *Let's Think!* (Adey, Robertson and Venville, 2001) and *Let's Think through Science!* (Adey *et al.*, 2003). Anne Robertson (with Michael Shayer and Mundher Adhami) wrote *Let's Think through Maths!* (2004).

Anne Robertson trained and worked as a primary school teacher in Edinburgh in the early 1970s before moving to Tottenham in 1981. She taught in Haringey and Newham until taking an advisory post in Barking and Dagenham. She started working in Hammersmith and Fulham in 1998, focusing on developing thinking with pupils. She now lectures at the Institute of Education and is the Course Leader for the full-time primary PGCE course.

Philip Adey is a Professor at King's College London and Director of the Centre for the Advancement of Thinking. Working as a teacher he became interested in the source of pupils' difficulties with learning, and this led him into studying cognitive development and acceleration.

At-a-Glance Guide to using Let's Think through Science! 8 & 9

This Guide contains everything you need to work through the 20 activities with a class of pupils in order to develop their thinking within the context of science. You may find it helpful to follow the steps below.

1 First, familiarise yourself with the materials by reading **Chapters 1 and 2**, which describe the approach taken.

2 **Chapter 3** shows how this resource translates theory into practice.

3 **Chapter 4** gives practical details on how to use the materials most effectively.

4 Choose the most appropriate **groupings** for your pupils using the guidelines on pages 8 and 9.

5 Select your **starting activity** by using the guidelines on page 11.

6 Read the **preparation** needed and the **step-by-step instructions** for that activity. These are found in the activity outlines on pages 15–61.

7 Photocopy the **resources** required for that activity using the Resource Section on pages 63–87.

8 Gather together any other resources required as described under the heading **Materials** at the start of each activity. Some of these may include resources that you have kept following a previous activity.

9 Prepare any **resources that are not supplied**. Instructions about what is needed are found in the activity outlines on pages 15–61.

10 Carry out the **activity** using the step-by-step instructions in the activity outlines on pages 15–61.

11 If the instructions recommend that you **keep the materials** for a subsequent activity, please do so. It is sometimes essential that pupils continue work begun in a previous activity, using the same resources.

ONE

Introduction

Why Let's Think through Science! is useful in the classroom

Let's Think through Science! 8 & 9 is the latest addition to a family of materials that help teachers to promote pupils' thinking abilities. However, it is also a stand-alone programme, and teachers need no experience of previous books in the series to use it to its full potential. Designed for use with eight- and nine-year-old pupils (Year 4 in England and Wales, P5 in Scotland), *Let's Think through Science! 8 & 9* has two main aims:

- to help pupils develop their general ability to think;
- to help them further to develop this thinking within the context of science.

Let's Think through Science! 8 & 9 combines the development of general thinking ability with attention to the particular types of thinking required to 'reach inside' the science topics typically included in curricula for eight- and nine-year-olds: this is a powerful approach. Science is as much a 'way of thinking' as it is a body of knowledge. Focusing on scientific ways of thinking will give pupils a deeper level of access to the content material.

Focus on science

The first *Let's Think!* programme (Adey, Robertson and Venville, 2001) helps five- and six-year-olds to develop their general thinking ability. The more recent additions to the series set cognitive acceleration more clearly in the context of science subject matter. *Let's Think through Science!* for seven- and eight-year-olds (Adey *et al.*, 2003) helps pupils to develop their thinking via science. *Let's Think through Maths!* (Shayer, Adhami and Robertson, 2004) helps five- and six-year-olds to develop their mathematical thinking.

Science in the early years of primary education has had a rocky history. There have been many good intentions and much excellent material produced. However, the impact of such materials on the practice of primary science education has, at best, been patchy. The prescription of science content in the form of national science curricula has probably done little to encourage high-quality constructive teaching of science. Teachers who have little background in the subject may have come to see the content as a set of details to be learned, rather than as an opportunity for exploring scientific thinking. The *Let's Think!* programmes set out to redress this balance, showing teachers a new way of working whilst still meeting the requirements of the curriculum.

Finding your way around the Teacher's Guide

The Teacher's Guide gives full support and guidance to teachers using *Let's Think through Science! 8 & 9*. Chapter 2 provides information about the theory of thinking. Chapter 3 shows how *Let's Think through Science! 8 & 9* translates theory into practice. General guidelines for using the activities in the classroom are provided in Chapter 4, which also provides a step-by-step guide on how to begin using the programme (see page 11). Chapter 5 describes how the programme was developed. Full instructions for each activity are given in Chapter 6.

The Resource Section at the back of this book contains photocopy masters for all the Resource sheets that you will need for the activities. Some of the activities also use common materials that you will already have in school, or could obtain or make easily.

The At-a-Glance Guide (which faces this page) provides you with a quick reference: it will help you to get an overview of the programme and remind you of how it should be used.

Now turn to Chapter 2 for essential information on why it is important to teach thinking, how thinking processes develop and how their development may be accelerated.

TWO

Theoretical Foundations

Intelligence is a respectable psychological construct that can be described more clearly and measured more reliably than many other constructs, such as motivation, personality or learning style. It is also a construct that has, at times, been misinterpreted. A small group of psychologists have described it as a fixed attribute, and one that is mostly inherited: as a result, intelligence has sometimes had a bad press. For this reason, some educators have become reluctant to accept the concept and are wary of even using the word. It is quite right that this view of intelligence should have fallen into disrepute, but to throw out the whole idea just because it has been misused by a few is counterproductive. This chapter begins by describing some of the key features of intelligence; it then goes on to describe the development of children's thinking, and how this can be maximised.

Features of intelligence

Two of the most important features of intelligence are that it can be applied across *all areas of academic learning* (in this sense it may be described as 'general thinking' ability) and that it can be *developed over time* (and is therefore 'educable'). These two features are described below. Both lie at the heart of most cognitive acceleration programmes.

General thinking ability

People with a well-developed 'general thinking' ability are particularly good at making mental connections. Although they may have a specific talent in one particular area (for example, number, language or music), an underlying 'general' intelligence factor is present. In day-to-day life, strong general thinking abilities are often indicated by the capacity to:

- see things from a different perspective (for example, a pupil with strong general thinking abilities will sometimes ask questions that take the teacher by surprise);
- recognise patterns in data;
- transfer knowledge from one context to another;
- go beyond the 'given';
- anticipate where an argument is going;
- be creative.

'Educability'

General thinking ability is not a fixed capacity that can be described once and for all by an intelligence quotient ('IQ') score, but one that is educable: it can be developed through education. Indeed, one of the main functions of schooling is to do just that: to maximise the intellectual capacity of every child. At this point it is useful to consider the way in which children's thinking abilities develop and how these abilities might best be nurtured.

The development of children's thinking

Jean Piaget (1896–1980) is well known for his belief that children's thinking develops through distinct stages. He also proposed that intellectual development is not simply a matter of learning *more* things, but of growing into *qualitatively different ways of thinking* about the observed world. Piaget and his co-workers reported hundreds of hours of detailed analysis of the thinking of children of different ages. This massive corpus of work provides a wonderfully rich resource for understanding cognitive development.

Piaget used the term 'concrete operations' to describe mental operations involving the world of material things. A concrete operation is a mental operation involving concrete reality and concrete operations skills are acquired over many years.

In broad terms, the whole phase of primary education, from around five to 11 years of age, corresponds to the period during which children are developing *concrete operations*. A concrete operation is a mental operation on concrete reality: for example, adding five beans to three beans and getting eight – consistently and reliably. This may seem rather simple, but for a child of, maybe, four years old who is not yet using concrete operations, the concrete world appears to be a surprisingly slippery place. For example, she may agree that two rows of beads have the same number, as one bead has been put in one row and a corresponding bead in the other row. But when we push the beads in one row close together, and spread those in the other row further apart, she will now claim that there are more beads in the longer row. This is *preoperational* thinking – the child is not yet able to use simple mental operations reliably in real situations. There is little in the concrete world that is perceived as constant.

A few children even at nine years old will find concrete operations difficult. These are likely to be children identified as having learning difficulties. At the other end of the scale, a few 10-year-olds will have started to deal comfortably with abstractions and multi-variable situations. These are gifted children who are moving into the stage of thinking typical of adolescents: *formal operations*. So concrete operations spans a wide age-range and growth through concrete operations involves becoming increasingly confident in dealing with situations that need four or five bits of information to be held at once in the active 'processing' space of the mind. There are clear differences between the types of thinking characteristic of early and late concrete operations. *Let's Think through Science! 8 & 9* is designed specifically to stimulate intellectual growth through concrete operations.

Stimulating the development of thinking abilities

How can we stimulate the growth of general thinking? In the 1980s, Piaget's idea that thinking develops through distinct stages fell into some disrepute because it was occasionally misused to identify what children could *not* do. The idea can also be used positively, however; understanding the type of thinking that individual children are using enables us to design activities that will move them on towards higher levels of thinking. This is the process that is described as 'cognitive acceleration'. There are three main drivers of cognitive acceleration – three conditions that work together to maximise the intellectual growth of children. These are described below.

Cognitive conflict

Piaget suggested that experiences that are puzzling to a child, and cannot be easily explained, may stimulate the development of more powerful ways of thinking. It can therefore be worthwhile to provide children with activities and experiences that challenge their current understanding and are somewhat difficult for them to solve at the moment. Of course, each activity has to be well managed and pitched at the correct level of difficulty, neither so easy that it provides no challenge, nor so difficult that it alienates the children.

Social construction

Faced with a problem, the natural human instinct is to talk about it – this is why, in the adult world, we frequently set up committees or 'think tanks' to solve problems. Our assumption is that 'many heads are better than one'. In some school settings, however, collaboration is viewed less positively; it may even be construed as 'cheating'. In cognitive acceleration, we actively encourage children to work together to solve problems. This process – 'social construction' of understanding – is recognised in psychology, the most well-known proponent of the idea being Lev Vygotsky (1896–1934).

Metacognition

The third driver for cognitive acceleration, derived indirectly from both Vygotsky and Piaget, is conscious 'thinking about your own thinking' – which is known as 'metacognition'. Active reflection on progress in solving a particular problem, on difficulties encountered, on wrong turns taken and how they were corrected, can stimulate the development of improved thinking.

Three pillars of cognitive acceleration

This approach to the stimulation of intelligence in children can be summarised as follows:

- provide a challenging activity (cognitive conflict);
- encourage a social approach to tackling it (social construction);
- help children to think back to the thinking they employed (metacognition).

Cognitive conflict, social construction and metacognition are collectively described as 'three pillars of cognitive acceleration'.

THREE

From Theory into Practice

The three pillars of cognitive acceleration, as described in Chapter 2, are theoretical. However, they have provided a useful framework for the development of *Let's Think through Science! 8 & 9* and other cognitive acceleration programmes.

Cognitive acceleration in the classroom

In moving from theory to practice, two further 'pillars' are needed to complete the model of cognitive acceleration: 'concrete preparation' and 'bridging'. These are described below.

Concrete preparation

Pupils cannot simply be thrown a new and difficult problem, then left alone to struggle. Instead, they need to be led towards it and introduced to it. You, the teacher will help them to establish:

- what the activity is about;
- what they already know about this topic;
- what new vocabulary will be used.

This phase is called 'concrete preparation', and it sets the scene for the problem.

Bridging

The thinking abilities developed during a particular activity need to be generalised for use in other contexts. Therefore the final 'pillar' of cognitive acceleration is identifying where else similar thinking can be used and applied; this is known as 'bridging'. In *Let's Think through Science! 8 & 9*, bridging does not necessarily come at the end of the activity; you may find opportunities for it at any time.

The five pillars of cognitive acceleration

The *Let's Think through Science! 8 & 9* activities will provide practical examples of all five pillars of cognitive acceleration in action:

- concrete preparation;
- cognitive conflict;
- social construction;
- metacognition;
- bridging.

An initial familiarity with the terms, and the opportunity to refer back to their definitions from time to time (above and on pages 3–4), will help you to understand:

- *why* the activities are the way that they are;
- *how* to teach *Let's Think through Science! 8 & 9*, since the method required is somewhat different from normal teaching practice (see also pages 10–11).

Concrete operations in practice

In Chapter 2 we described Piaget's definition of 'concrete operations' as the 'mental operations involving the world of material things'. *Let's Think through Science! 8 & 9* promotes this type of thinking; it is designed specifically to stimulate intellectual growth through concrete operations. Here we will describe in a little more detail some of the different kinds of thinking that comprise concrete operations.

The word *schema* (plural *schemata*) is used to describe a general way of thinking that can be applied in many different contexts. If pupils did not develop schemata, they would be condemned to devising a new solution each time they encountered a familiar problem in an unfamiliar situation, whether or not they had solved it before in a different context.

Some examples of concrete schemata are described below, together with examples of the type of activity that each schema needs. *Let's Think through Science! 8 & 9* provides activities that will help pupils to develop thinking abilities related to all six of these schemata.

Classification

Even elementary work on living and non-living things requires pupils to put them into groups with some characteristics in common: that is, to classify them. *Classification* problems can be graded in difficulty according to how many variables are involved, how many values each variable has, and how clearly the different groups are defined. A *variable* is simply a way in which things vary from one another. For example, they may vary in colour, in shape, or ways of moving. Colour, shape and ways of moving are all variables. Each variable may have a number of values. The variable 'colour' may have the *values* blue, green, red, etc. The variable 'ways of moving' may have values walk, fly, swim, and so on.

Causality

Causality is a special type of relationship between variables. What causes what? We may laugh if we hear a young child say that the wind is caused by the trees waving back and forth, and yet from the perspective of a three- or four-year-old child, this may be a perfectly reasonable conclusion. The confusion of *Correlation* (things happening together) with *Causality* (one making the other happen) is a problem that besets even some supposedly intelligent adults. A classic example is the belief that 'larger classes get higher grades'. This may be the case, but does it follow that we should therefore increase class sizes to improve grades? In *Let's Think through Science! 8 & 9* pupils explore *Causality* in a variety of contexts, such as the relationship between the brightness of a light and the elements controlling that brightness (**Activity 6.3: Controlling the Light**), and the relationship between animals and habitat (**Activity 2.2: How am I Adapted?**).

Seriation

Seriation means putting things in order. In the first *Let's Think!* pack (Adey, Robertson and Venville, 2001), five- and six-year-old pupils are set the task of putting 10 sticks in order of length. This provides considerable cognitive conflict for five-year-olds, but would be too easy for most eight- and nine-year-olds. In **Activity 3.3: I like my Soup Hot**, pupils have to order materials in terms of how good an insulator they are – which is quite difficult. The point is to develop the *general* ability to order things; *Seriation* skills can be used in many different contexts.

Concrete modelling

Concrete modelling is the building of simple models that offer an explanation for observations; each element of the model has a specific concrete referent. In **Activity 1.3: What makes me Move?**, for example, pupils are encouraged to develop a concrete model showing how bones, joints and muscles work together to effect movement.

Relationship between variables

'The bigger the bone, the stronger it is.' Is that true? In other words, is there a relationship between the variable 'size of the bone' and the variable 'strength of the bone'? Science is all about exploring relationships between variables; therefore, some of the activities in this programme give pupils an opportunity to do just that (see **Activity 3.2: Hotter or Colder?** and **Activity 5.3: Late for School**).

Conservation

The fact that a quantity of water remains the same when you pour it from one container to another is obvious to adults, but not to some eight-year-olds. In order to become aware of 'conserved' quantities, one has to develop the schema of *Conservation*: an understanding that the *amount* of many materials stays the same, even though their *shape* or *location* has been changed.

Understanding that the volume of water remains the same when it is moved to a differently shaped container (when, for example, it is poured from a short fat measuring jug into a tall thin glass) requires the pupil to see that the greater height of the water level is compensated for by the fact that the container is narrower. This requires considerable mental processing. As adults, we have taken this fact for granted for many years, we are therefore surprised at how difficult it is for some eight-year-olds to grasp. **Activity 4.2: I can't find the Sugar** uses this schema.

These six schemata, or 'ways of thinking', underlie all scientific thought and much general thinking as well.

FOUR

Using Let's Think through Science! 8 & 9

This chapter provides some general guidance for teachers aiming to develop pupils' general thinking ability through science. From the account of the five pillars, described in Chapters 2 and 3, it will be clear that the teacher has a particular role during these activities. This is described below alongside some general considerations for using *Let's Think through Science! 8 & 9* with eight- and nine-year-old pupils (Year 4 in England and Wales, P5 in Scotland).

What does the programme consist of?

The programme comprises 20 activities based on various topics within the science curricula that are typically taught to eight- and nine-year-old pupils. The selected topics are:

- Moving and growing;
- Habitats;
- Keeping warm;
- Solids and liquids;
- Friction;
- Circuits and conductors.

Each of the activities addresses one or more of the schemata of concrete operations, as follows:

- *Classification*;
- *Causality*;
- *Seriation*;
- *Concrete modelling*;
- *Relationship between variables*;
- *Conservation*.

The key features of each schema are outlined in a Schema Fact Box. It is important that you read this explanation carefully, so that you become familiar with the underlying type of thinking being developed in a particular set of activities. A description of each schema is also included in Chapter 3.

Within each topic the activities appear in a suggested order, but the order of the topics is not important.

When is the programme used?

It is suggested that each activity should take the place of an hour-long science lesson. If one *Let's Think through Science! 8 & 9* activity is taught every two weeks, there is time within the school year to complete the whole programme. If you prefer, however, you can follow the example of those schools that teach topics over a two-year cycle: *Let's Think through Science!* for seven- and eight-year-olds and *Let's Think through Science! 8 & 9* are designed for use during the two years, as appropriate to each school's curriculum map. If your class is in the seven to eight years age group when these topics are taught (Year 3 in England and Wales; P4 in Scotland), the activities are still relevant and can still develop pupils' thinking.

How should the pupils be grouped?

Let's Think through Science! 8 & 9 is designed for use with *all* the pupils in a class, working in separate groups of four. The pupils within each group should be mixed according to ability, gender, ethnicity and personality. Sometimes the pupils are required to work with a partner so it is helpful if they are divided into pairs within each group. The aim is to make these groups into genuine mini-discussion groups. Avoid seeing the groups simply as four pupils working separately at the same table; view each pupil as one individual contributing to the whole. The pupils should be encouraged to listen to each group member, making eye contact where possible. They may need help in respecting each opinion and contribution while at the same time recognising that not every idea will be agreed upon and used to solve the particular challenge. Acceptable ways of rejecting ideas may need to be taught, explained and tried out. When the pupils embark on the main activities they will then be more ready to collaborate, and to verbalise and be challenged on their reasoning.

Groups for the introductory activities

Choosing the groups within your class is very important to the future success of the programme. At the beginning of the term, as you get to know the pupils, various combinations can be tried in different groups.

The two introductory activities (A and B) have been included to help you decide on the groupings for your class. Activities A and B are suggested, but other short challenges or puzzles could be used. As the pupils work on these activities, you are establishing rules for working together and helping them to deal with situations where some need extra support.

Groups for the main activities

Once you begin to use the main activities, it is recommended that the pupils are not shifted from group to group. Pupils generally pick up negative messages if they are moved around, so this should be avoided as much as possible. Difficulties within a group can be addressed, often with the teacher's help, so that pupils can work at resolving problems. This may be difficult in the short term, but is beneficial to long-term emotional maturity and healthy interpersonal relationships.

How should the classroom be arranged?

It is helpful for the class discussion if the tables can be arranged in such a way that the pupils are able to make as much eye contact as possible, both with those pupils in their own group and with their classmates in other groups. This encourages them to challenge and question each other rather than being tempted to 'talk through the teacher'.

The phases of a Let's Think through Science! 8 & 9 activity

Using the Detailed Guidelines

The Detailed Guidelines provided in Chapter 6 (pages 15–61) are not intended to be prescriptive. Each activity will be different and you will often need to make changes to your own plan in response to the way the activity is developing. Where possible, the Guidelines provide some approximate timings for each phase, but you may find that the actual time spent varies widely.

Follow the structure of each activity, whilst at the same time making the activity your own. Remember that 'getting to the end of the activity' is not the main focus. Begin by establishing what the activity is about and what the pupils already know about the topic (see *Concrete preparation*, page 5). Then concentrate on ensuring that the pupils:

- are challenged (see the section on *Cognitive conflict*, page 3);
- are given the opportunity for group and class discussion (see *Social construction*, page 3);
- have time to reflect on their own learning (see *Metacognition*, page 3): if time is running out, it is important to stop the group activity and make time for this.

You should also include *Bridging* within the activity (see page 5). Ensure that the pupils make appropriate links, both *forward* to areas in which they might be able to use similar thinking in the future and *back* to other work that they have done in the past. If the pupils have engaged with the activity and are working well in their groups, you may be tempted to let the activity run on beyond the allotted hour. Try to avoid this temptation so that the class can benefit more fully from all aspects of the programme.

Concrete preparation

In a *Let's Think through Science! 8 & 9* activity you will find yourself moving back and forth between whole-class and small-group discussions. The 'concrete preparation' phase is normally a whole-class session, in which you establish what today's activity is about, introducing any new words, and generally 'setting the scene'. Try not to prolong the concrete preparation phase unduly. It is the part of the *Let's Think through Science! 8 & 9* activity that is most like 'normal' teaching, and there may be a temptation to hang on to the relative familiarity of this mode.

Cognitive conflict and social construction

In the next phase, you need pupils to move into groups of four to work on the activity. Walk round the classroom and observe the pupils as they work. Occasionally pose a question; challenge those groups that think they have completed the task; monitor as far as possible the quality of the discussion and the inclusion of every individual. Remember that your principal role at this stage is that of 'listener'.

At any time you may ask for the attention of the whole class and suggest that one or two groups share their findings or any questions or disagreements that have arisen: you will certainly need to do so towards the end of this phase. The purpose here is not to reach a resolution, but to spread the challenges as widely as possible and maximise the process of social construction. Listen attentively to the pupils' findings, but make little comment – and certainly no evaluation. Where there are differences between groups, ask each to explain and justify their position more fully, and ask other groups to enter the discussion. Sometimes it is a matter of 'different ways of saying the same thing', but there may be genuine differences.

Remember that your aim here is to maximise the cognitive conflict and social construction, not to drive the pupils towards a 'right' answer.

Metacognition

After some time working on the problem and developing ideas, you should try to generate some metacognition. Encourage the pupils to think back to the problems they encountered and how they overcame them. Depending on how you choose to direct the activity, this might lead to the exploration of new problems and a new cycle of group work, whole-class social construction and metacognition.

Are special methods required for teaching Let's Think through Science! 8 & 9?

By now you will have realised that teaching for the stimulation of thinking may require different teaching methods from those employed in your normal curriculum work.

Shifting your philosophy

During the *Let's Think through Science! 8 & 9* activities you often need something of a shift in philosophy from being a 'leading' teacher, anxious to ensure that pupils receive all the help they need, to one who sets difficult problems and gives pupils more responsibility for finding their own solutions. This does not mean that you simply sit back and watch them struggle. Your role becomes that of a 'mediator', asking open questions that progress pupils' thinking without providing them with answers. Your modelling of this role of mediation encourages pupils to begin to adopt it themselves in order to help other members of their group. Also you are trying to ensure that all pupils experience some cognitive conflict while listening and contributing to the search for a combined solution. This is challenging work.

Characteristics of the 'listening' teacher

During group work, your role is mainly to *listen* – so as to retain important ideas, explanations and questions that the pupils are discussing. When it comes to the class discussion, you will then be able to ask specific questions of particular groups, so that the main points emerge. As you listen, it is useful if you do *not* repeat what individual pupils say for the benefit of others; it is important that all the members of the class learn to listen carefully to their peers.

Here are some other characteristics of the teacher who is helping pupils to develop their thinking abilities. He or she will:

- suspend judgement, leaving pupils to make up their own minds;
- encourage pupils to listen to one another with respect;
- understand 'mistakes' as opportunities to learn;
- help groups learn to share their thinking with the class;
- accept inconclusive or uncertain endings: it is the thinking along the way that matters;
- rarely 'tell', frequently ask and always respect;
- test ideas with pupils, working towards a consensus but accepting differences;
- allow time for reflection on 'how we got to this point'.

Just two final points. First, this is a special kind of teaching for intellectual stimulation. It would not be practicable to use this mode of teaching all the time, but it does provide an extra set of skills to add to your pedagogical armoury. Secondly, it takes time to develop these skills: you can expect to get worse before you get better. So persevere through the 'implementation dip', and give yourself time to develop your practice.

When should I start using the programme?

You can begin using *Let's Think through Science! 8 & 9* at any time. It does not matter if you do not start at the beginning of the school year. Simply choose from the list on page 15 a topic that corresponds to the subject area you are currently working on in science lessons.

How do I start?

- Divide your class into groups of four pupils, bearing in mind the suggestions above and on pages 8–9.
- Depending on your class and how much experience the pupils already have of group work, you may need to allow some time for discussion as to how a group can best operate successfully. Having established the ground rules, you are ready to begin. Give pupils a group challenge (such as Introductory Activity A). Observe whether the pupils work well together in their groups and check that the groups are well balanced in terms of different personality types, gender balance, etc.
- Make any necessary changes to the groupings.
- Use another introductory activity (such as Introductory Activity B) to give the pupils a chance to practise following the guidelines for effective group work.
- Finalise your groupings, and avoid changing them for the rest of the school year.
- Choose from the list on page 15 a topic that corresponds to the subject area you are currently working on in science lessons.
- Read *Concrete preparation for group working* on page 20 before you start your chosen topic.
- Work through your chosen topic, allowing one hour for each activity. **Keep to the suggested order of activities**. Questions, instructions and prompts that you may find useful in the classroom are displayed **in bold text**.
- Continue in this way throughout the school year, choosing topics as you wish.

What if I need more guidance?

This Teacher's Guide provides full detailed instructions on how to use the programme. Teachers, schools and local education authorities are also invited to contact:

Anne Robertson
Course Leader for Full-time PGCE
Early Childhood and Primary Education
Institute of Education
20 Bedford Way
London WC14 0AL
telephone: 020 7612 6235
e-mail: a.robertson@ioe.ac.uk

Phillip Adey
Science Department
Institute of Education
20 Bedford Way
London WC14 0AL
telephone: 020 7612 6235
e-mail: p.adey@ioe.ac.uk

FIVE

How the Let's Think through Science! Programmes were Developed

The CASE and CAME projects

Since 1984, researchers at King's College London have been investigating the process of 'cognitive acceleration' – the promotion of higher-level thinking. The first main project was Cognitive Acceleration through Science Education (CASE), which was funded by the Economic and Social Research Council (1984–87). The project was set in a science context and aimed at 10- to 14-year-olds. Cognitive Acceleration through Mathematics Education (CAME), which focused first on 10- to 14-year-olds, and then on the upper primary years, was developed during the period 1993–97.

Although related to particular subject areas and taught (in secondary schools) by the relevant subject teachers, neither CASE nor CAME made any attempt to cover the content of any particular science or mathematics curriculum. They were squarely aimed at the development of general thinking, using the subject areas as convenient contexts for this purpose.

CATE and the ARTS Project

Since then, at secondary school level, there has been research conducted in a technology context: Cognitive Acceleration Techniques in Technology Education (CATE) by Tony Hamaker. The Arts Reasoning and Thinking Skills (ARTS) Project was a three-year action research project set up by Wigan local education authority.

CASE@KS1 (Let's Think!)

In 1998, the research team started working with five- and six-year-olds on a project originally called CASE@KS1, later published as *Let's Think!* (Adey, Robertson and Venville, 2001). This name reflects the principal aim of the materials – to promote thinking ability: their connections with science are not direct.

Let's Think through Science!

The first *Let's Think through Science!* (Adey *et al.*, 2003), which was designed for seven- and eight-year-olds, and this version for eight- and nine-year-olds, share many of the foundations on which their predecessors were based, such as:

- a sharp focus on the development of better thinking;
- a psychological model based on the work of Piaget and Vygotsky;
- some of the general teaching methods that arise from this model.

But the two *Let's Think though Science!* programmes also have their own characteristics that distinguish them from other members of the family, the most obvious of which is their close alignment with the content matter typical of science curricula for the relevant age range.

The research team's method of working was as follows:

- First, the team members re-engaged themselves with the general methods of cognitive acceleration (described in Chapter 3).
- The team then identified a set of topics common in the science curriculum in Years 3 and 4.
- The National Curriculum for England Scheme of Work for science was used for this purpose, but the topics covered in both programmes are typical of many other science curricula designed for seven- to nine-year-olds.

- Some chosen topics were analysed in order to identify the types of general cognitive processing they required.
- The team drafted a set of activities that would set the cognitive acceleration principles squarely in science topic contexts.
- The draft activities were tried with 20 Year 4 classes during the academic year 2001–02.

Finally extensive trialling again took place during the school year 2002–03, with a different 20 classes. Classroom observation and meetings with the teachers took place in order to evaluate the materials in terms of their:

- practicability and usefulness for busy teachers;
- effects on pupils;
- potential for providing cognitive stimulation, while at the same time remaining recognisably related to the science curriculum.

What is presented here is the result of editing of the activities based on trials in the London Boroughs of Hammersmith and Fulham, and Harrow.

Evidence of the benefits of Let's Think through Science!

In the trial schools in Hammersmith and Fulham and in Harrow, teachers and pupils were overwhelmingly positive about these methods of teaching. Positive effects can be seen by accessing schools' Ofsted reports: these refer directly to the programme, and to pupils' use of talk, questioning and collaboration.

Finally, here are some of the many very positive remarks made by teachers in response to the questions on their final feedback forms at the end of the trialling.

How has this programme affected your classroom practice?

- 'I was always nervous of teaching science, but now I have learnt to let the pupils discuss more openly without my intervention.'
- 'When I joined the programme, I ... enjoyed teaching science but ... wanted to give the answers. It has helped me to develop my questioning skills and my ability to encourage pupils to think for themselves.'
- 'I don't settle for a "yes" or "no" answer so often now: I like to ask them "Why?" or "How?"'
- 'It has enhanced my ability to maintain an open, comfortable learning environment where the pupils feel safe in expressing their ideas.'
- 'My expectations of the students have led to me teaching science with great enthusiasm.'
- 'It has helped me to encourage pupils to reflect on what they say and to verbalise their thoughts/reasoning.'
- 'I feel I now give *all* my students, instead of just the ones with their hands up, a greater opportunity to share their own ideas.'
- 'I feel like a better teacher.'

Has the programme had any effect on your pupils' learning and social behaviour?

- 'They are more ready to learn from each other rather than seeing this as "copying ideas".'
- 'They are more willing to comment on what others have said and challenge ideas that they don't agree with.'
- 'Their understanding and acceptance of the importance of listening has really improved.'
- 'Pupils are more aware of how they reached a decision or changed their mind.'
- 'They are more able to express themselves, not so worried about right or wrong answers.'
- 'They enjoy talking about themselves as "thinkers".'
- 'Pupils who lack ability and confidence, in areas such as literacy, have been able to demonstrate their intelligence verbally, which has possibly changed their [peer perceptions].'
- 'The high-ability pupils in my class have been stretched in ways that they don't always experience in day-to-day lessons.'

- 'Generally there is a greater willingness to work cooperatively in groups and they have learned ways of doing this without killing each other!'
- 'I have seen evidence of pupils working together and cooperating as a "group" – bringing to light the difference between this and sitting at the same table in a group of six, which we often say is group work but actually involves very little real interaction.'
- 'I believe that it has helped one particular child in my class who had problems with social interaction – particularly as he no longer responds aggressively when other pupils disagree with him.'

Research into measuring the effects that *Let's Think through Science!* for seven- and eight-year-olds and *Let's Think through Science! 8 & 9* have on pupils' cognitive and scientific development, and also the impact that the related professional development has on teachers' classroom practice, is currently being carried out. Analysis of the quantitative and qualitative data produced from this will be made available once the research is complete.

Please note: A further member of the *Let's Think!* family – *Let's Think through Maths!* (Shayer, Adhami and Robertson, 2004) – is designed for use with Key Stage 1 (P1–P3) pupils, to develop their thinking in mathematics.

SIX

Detailed Guidelines for Use

List of activities

Materials

The Resource Section at the back of this book (see page 63) contains photocopy masters for all the Resource sheets that you will need for the activities. Some of the activities also use common materials that you will already have in school, or could obtain or make easily. In order to keep the cost of the resource down, these have not been supplied.

Introductory activity Activity A

Climb that Mountain

Aim

The pupils are presented with an activity that gives them the opportunity to think systematically through a problem by means of group discussion, as they will be required to do in the activities that follow. The pupils also become more conscious of the techniques and strategies that make for effective group working. In addition, you, the teacher, have the opportunity to observe the groups and see whether you need to make any adjustments to their composition.

Materials

Supplied

- Resource sheet 1, which shows a mountain with three peaks and many stepping-stones leading to them. Each stepping-stone is labelled with a number between 0 and 9.

Before you start

Take photocopies of Resource sheet 1 – one copy for each group.

Activity

Cognitive conflict and social construction

- Explain to the pupils that they will be given an activity to do, and that they will have 10–15 minutes to complete it in their groups. They can use any means to solve the problem but at the end they need to be able to explain how they did it.
- Ask the groups to begin at the word '**Start**' and to climb to the top of the mountain by moving from stone to stone. Each step is worth the number of points on each stone. The object is to get to the top quickly, making the highest possible number of points on the way. The groups can move sideways as well as upwards. The group to make the most points in climbing to the top of any peak in the given time is the winning group. Pupils have to work out the best route in terms of time and points.
- After 10–15 minutes, ask each group to share their responses. If there are points of disagreement between groups, encourage whole-class discussion on how to resolve them.

Metacognition

- If all the groups solve the problem without any difficulty, look confused and say that you thought it was possible to make a higher number of points. Give them the opportunity to show you the method they would use to prove you wrong. **What did you have to think about to solve this? What did you discuss? Were there ideas that you decided not to follow? Why was this?** Encourage each group to listen and add to other groups' explanations.
- Ask the pupils to discuss how the members of their group worked together. **Were you happy in your group? Did your group work well? What made your group work well? What worked less well? How could that be changed to make things better next time?**

Reiterate the main behaviours that help to make a group work well, reminding the pupils that they should:

- **listen to each other;**
- **think about the ideas suggested and decide which to try;**
- **speak in a voice that the whole group can hear;**
- **ask when something is not clear.**

Also remind the pupils, **If you disagree with someone, explain your reasons so that the person understands.**

You may notice that some groups are not well balanced – for example, in terms of the personality types within the group. If so, note any changes that you will need to make before embarking on the next activity in about a week's time.

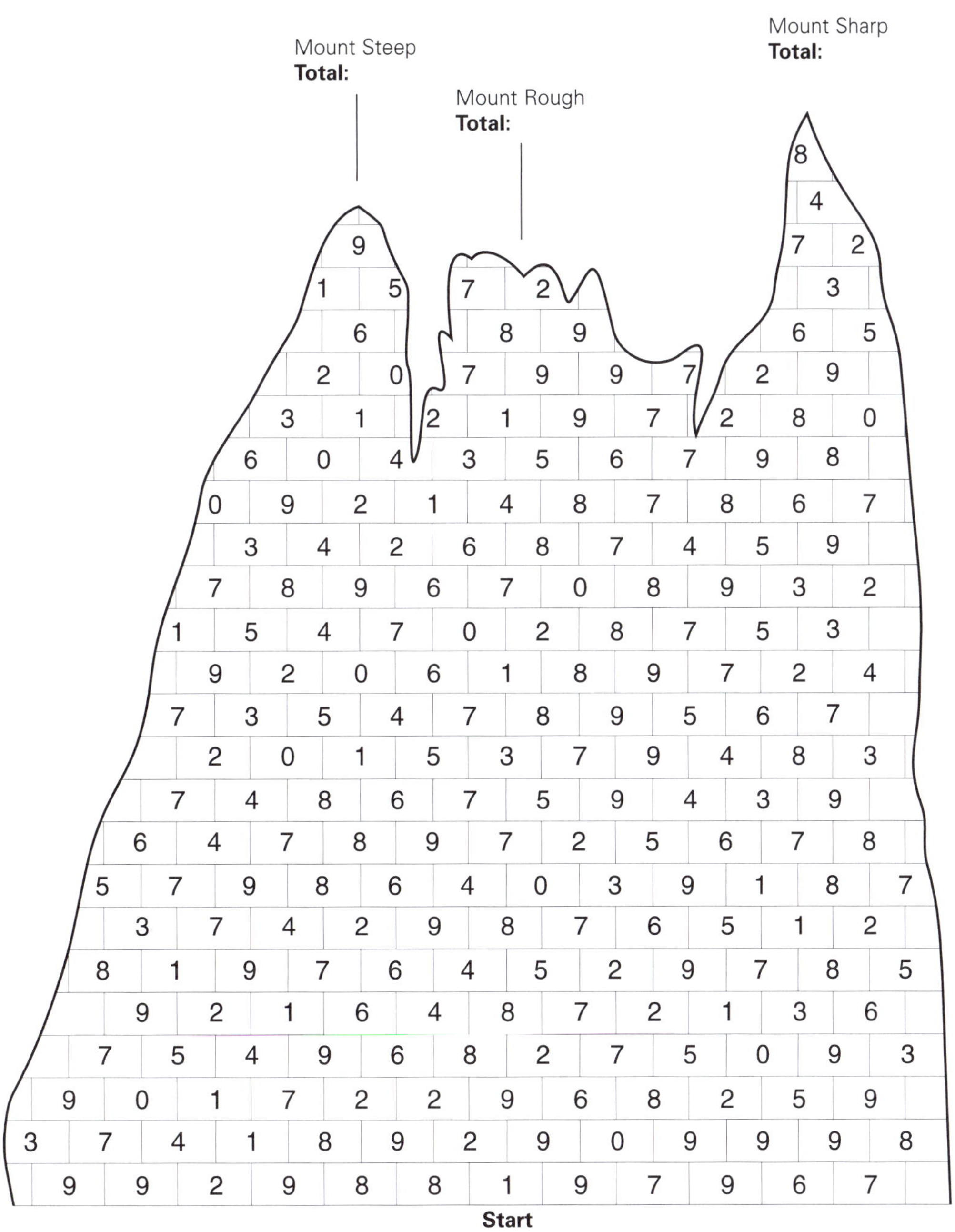

Introductory activity **Activity B**

Make that Box

Aim

The pupils are given a second opportunity to practise working effectively together in groups. The activity shows them that there is not always a single 'correct' answer to a problem and that there may instead be many possible solutions.

Materials

Supplied

- Resource sheet 2, which is a photocopiable page showing 24 cylinders, all exactly the same. The diameter of each cylinder is labelled 2cm. The height of each cylinder is labelled 5cm.

Not supplied

- For each group, a selection of thin card (A3 size), scissors, glue, staplers and rulers.

Before you start

Take photocopies of Resource sheet 2 – one for each group. Also give each group a selection of materials including: thin card, scissors, glue, a stapler and a ruler.

You may also wish to make an overhead projector transparency (OHT) of the Resource sheet, for use in the *Cognitive conflict and social construction* section.

Health and safety

Remind the pupils that scissors and staplers can be dangerous. Tell the pupils to use them carefully.

Activity

Concrete preparation

- Explain to the class that you are going to work through another group activity.
- Divide the class into groups of 4, taking account of last week's experience.
- Once the pupils are sitting in their groups, ask them what they remember from the last time about what helps a group to work. Encourage them to give reasons for how and why these behaviours help the group.
- As before, while the pupils are working in the groups, listen and evaluate whether this will make a good working combination of pupils. It is hoped that after this second experience you will be able to choose the final groups of 4, which will then stay in that combination for the rest of the year during *Let's Think through Science! 8 & 9* activities. It can also be very useful to use these groups for other activities, e.g. music, PE, history.

Cognitive conflict and social construction

- Give each group one photocopy of Resource sheet 2, showing the 24 cylinders.
- Tell the pupils: **I need to make a box that holds these containers. The box needs to fit tightly, so that the containers do not move about. You have to work out what size of box I need. Once you have agreed on the length of the sides you can try to make it together. You can use the box to help you explain how the containers will fit in the box**. Remind the pupils that at the end of the activity they will have to explain how they have gone about it.

- While the pupils are working, you can use this time to evaluate whether the groups now represent a good mix of abilities, gender, personalities, language skills, etc.
- After 15–20 minutes, ask each group to show their box to the class. So that everybody can see, it may be better to bring the whole class together, but ask the pupils to sit near to the other members of their group so that they can refer to each other. It may help to display a copy of the cylinder page on an overhead projector screen or on the whiteboard.
- Give the class a few minutes to look at each completed box. Meanwhile, think about how and why each group has reached its decision.
- **Are all the boxes the same? What differences do you notice? Are you happy with those? Why? Are there any differences you are not happy about? Why?**
- ***Please note:* There is no single 'correct' answer to this activity.** There are various possible arrangements of cylinders within the box, as shown below, and the 'best' arrangement may depend on use, function, place of storage, etc.

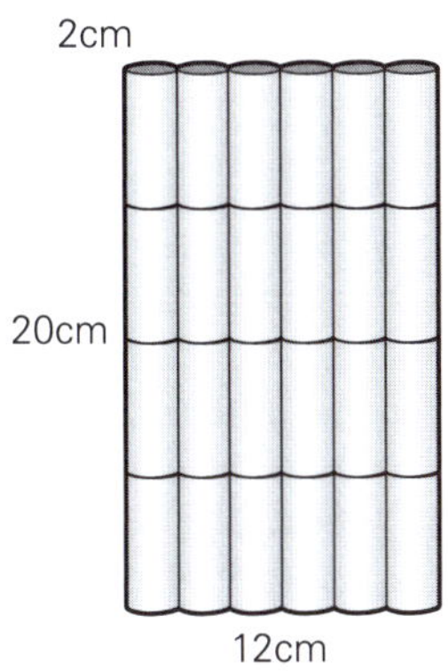

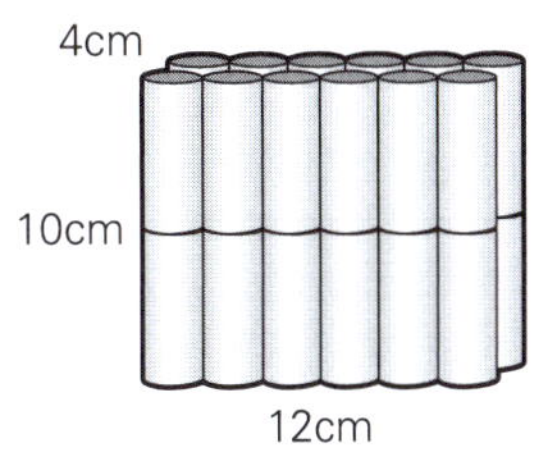

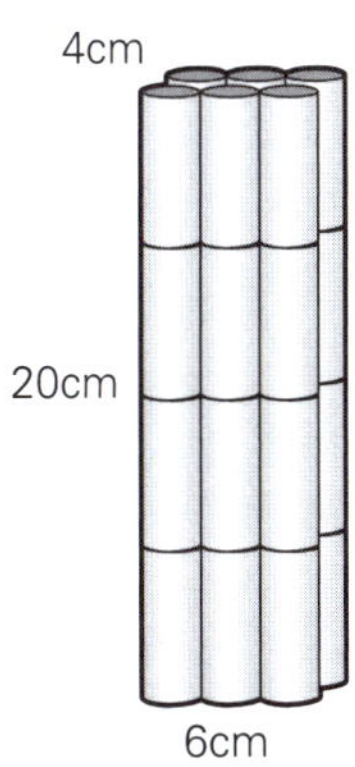

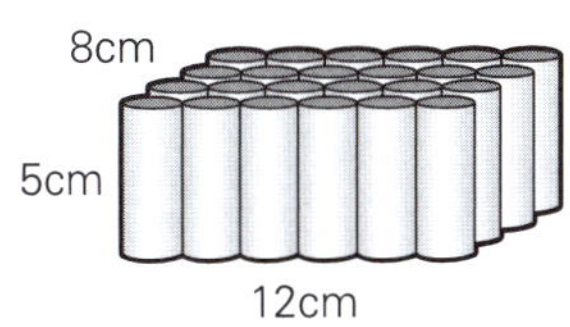

Metacognition

- Encourage the pupils to discuss any box where they think the cylinders will not fit. They must give a reason and say what the group could do to make a better fit. **How did you decide what your box should measure? What kind of thinking were you doing? Were all your ideas used? Why? What ways of thinking helped you best?**
- Ask them to discuss what it was like working in the group this week, as compared to last week. **Was it better? Why? Were there any difficulties? If so, how could they be resolved?**
- You should now be ready to finalise your groups for the *Let's Think through Science! 8 & 9* activities.
- Remember: if difficulties emerge within the groups during the year, it is better that these difficulties are expressed within the group and addressed rather than moving pupils to other groups. Issues of this nature will be discussed during the professional development attached to the programme (see page 11 for author contact details).

Schema

FACT BOX

Classification

ACTIVITIES 1.1 1.2 2.1 3.1 4.1 6.2

Introduction

To understand pupils' difficulties with the process of *Classification*, you need to understand two ideas: variables and values. A *variable* is simply a way in which things vary from one another. Colour, shape, and number of legs are all variables. Each variable may have a number of values. The variable 'colour' may have the *values* blue, green, red, etc. *Classification* problems become more difficult for pupils as the number of variables increases, and as the number of values of each variable increases.

Aim

Even elementary work on living and non-living things requires them to be put into groups with some characteristics in common: that is, to be classified. *Classification* problems can be graded in difficulty according to how many variables are involved, how many values each variable has, and how clearly defined each set is within the classification.

Activity 1.1: Who am I? invites the pupils to make links between the shapes of animals and their skeletons.

Activity 1.2: All these Bones requires the pupils to classify different human bones according to various criteria, e.g. shape, function, strength.

Activity 2.1: Where do I Live? requires the pupils to classify animals according to their native habitats.

Activity 3.1: How Hot are You? invites the pupils to classify scenarios according to given temperatures and match these to the thermometers given.

Activity 4.1: Where does it Belong? asks the pupils to consider criteria for grouping various substances while thinking about solids and liquids.

Activity 6.2: Do I Work? is an activity where pupils identify those circuits that make a bulb light up.

Moving and growing **Activity 1.1**

Who am I?

Aim

Pupils are challenged to identify pictures of skeletons of various animals. They classify the skeletons into groups according to their own chosen criteria. Pupils notice similarities and differences in size, shape and functions. They will develop some of these initial observations further through other activities during this topic.

Materials

Supplied

Resource sheets 3 to 6, which are all photocopiable pages, each with drawings of four or five animal skeletons. The skeletons are identified below, for your reference. ***Please note:* You should not reveal this information to the pupils in advance of the activity.**

- Resource sheet 3: 1: human, 2: fish, 3: dog, 4: bird.
- Resource sheet 4: 5: tiger, 6: heron, 7: ape, 8: horse.
- Resource sheet 5: 9: goat, 10: frog, 11: hare, 12: dinosaur.
- Resource sheet 6: 13: human baby, 14: child, 15: alligator, 16: snake, 17: parrot.

Before you start

Take photocopies of Resource sheets 3, 4, 5 and 6, one copy of each sheet for every group. Then cut up the sheets to make 4 sets of cards for each group.

You may also wish to make OHTs of the Resource sheets, for use in the concrete preparation for the activity.

Concrete preparation for group working

- Divide the pupils into their groups of 4 – having worked through the introductory activities you should by now have decided on the best possible configuration for these groups.
- Tell the pupils that they are going to do an activity in their groups. Discuss the kinds of behaviours that will help the groups to achieve the task. They may know that everybody in the group needs to be involved, that they need to speak and listen to each other, respect each other, etc. As they begin, however, they may forget some of these points and you may need to stop them occasionally to discuss what is happening.
- It may be useful for the pupils to think of allocating roles as a strategy, e.g. leader, scribe. It is more effective if they come up with this idea themselves. Tell them that at the end you may ask any of them to explain what went on in the group, regardless of their role in the group. As the pupils work, try not to engage with any group, but listen and observe how they are getting on together.

Activity

Concrete preparation for the activity

- Give each group the two sets of cards you have made by cutting up the photocopies of Resource sheets 3 and 4: these cards are numbered 1 to 8. Ask the groups to identify what animals they think the skeletons belong to and give the pupils time to discuss their ideas.
- After about 5 minutes, ask the groups to share what they think. If you wish, you could write the names of the animals on OHTs of each of the two Resource sheets. If more than one animal name is suggested for a particular skeleton, write them all down on the sheet. The pupils can then debate which one they think is more likely to be right, giving reasons for their choice. **Why do you think that? What clues are you using? Can you explain what led you to that conclusion?**

Cognitive conflict and social construction: Part 1

- Give each group the two sets of cards you have made by cutting up the photocopies of Resource sheets 5 and 6: these cards are numbered 9 to 17. Ask the pupils if they can name these skeletons. This should now be easier as a result of the first discussion and will only take a few minutes. Any discrepancies will be highlighted during the discussion about groupings.
- Ask the pupils to put all the 17 skeletons into groups. They will need to agree reasons for their choices. Pupils work together in their groups to classify the skeletons.
- Walk around the groups listening to their conversations. Occasionally, you can ask a question. Mostly, though, you should leave the pupils to engage with one other.
- After about 10 minutes, ask each group how they classified the skeletons.
- ***Class sharing:*** **What groups did you put the skeletons into? Why did you choose to put those together?**
- Tell the pupils to put all the skeletons back into the centre of their table and classify them in a different way: that is, using different criteria. Each group reclassifies the skeletons. Again, allow a few minutes for the groups to explain their new criteria.

  Here are some examples of groupings that pupils came up with:
  - all have four legs
  - all have two legs
  - all have no legs
  - all that can fly
  - all that can swim
  - all that can run
  - humans/not humans.

Metacognition (Whole class)

- Encourage the pupils to step back from the task and try to explain their thinking. Ask questions to make the thinking more conscious. **What kind of thinking have you been doing? What was making this task difficult? What helped you to sort out some of the problems? Did anybody say anything that particularly helped you?** This provides a good opportunity for the pupils to reflect on their decision-making process. They may also notice that some groups worked better than others. Again, this can be discussed. **What made your group work well?** They make comments such as: *We all listened to everyone. We shared our ideas. We thought about which one to follow. We had to agree and then try to follow the idea.* The groups that did not work so well can reflect on what aspect they did not manage. They can concentrate on developing this skill.

Cognitive conflict and social construction: Part 2

- Encourage the pupils to discuss similarities and differences between skeletons. **What do you notice that is the same about these skeletons? What differences do you notice? Why do you think there are these differences? What results do these differences lead to in terms of how these animals live?**
- Give the pupils 5–10 minutes to discuss these issues in their groups. Encourage class discussion of their ideas. Ask them to look at the human and the monkey. **What are the similarities and differences between these two? Why do you think this is? Do you think these skeletons have always looked like this? Think about the first humans we know about. Did their skeletons look like this? What are the differences? Why do you think this is?**
- Encourage all pupils to express what they think, listen to each other and make responses as a result of what they have heard. Encourage them to question and challenge each other.
- Be conscious of any religious beliefs that may be challenged by the scientific ideas. Handle this sensitively.

Metacognition

- **We are going to think about our thinking now. Think about what you had to do together to solve this challenge. What did you have to think about before you could decide what groups to put the skeletons into? What was difficult about this task? What helped you to do this? Is there anything you have learnt from this that you think you could use in another task?**
- Encourage the pupils to explain some of the ideas they discussed, some that caused disagreement, some that they could not resolve. **Have you changed your mind about anything? What is important about disagreeing? What enabled you to do this?** It is important for the pupils to realise that it is a crucial aspect of learning that they can evaluate their own ideas in the light of others. They need to remain open to changing their minds if they understand and accept the new idea. Thus they learn something new. They also need to know that if they do not accept the other idea, they can hold onto their original one: they may be right!
- Finish by asking the pupils to record 5 questions in their groups. **Ask 5 questions about skeletons – things that you may want to find out about as we do this topic**. Display these questions in a visible place for use in future activities.

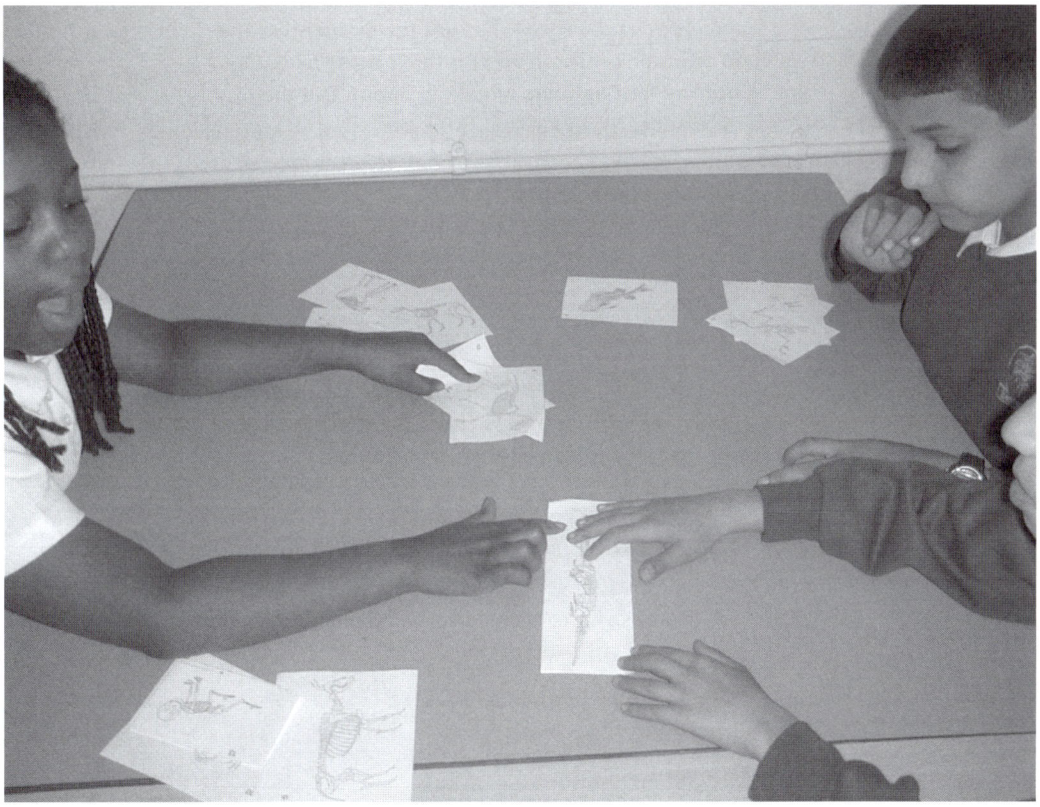

Schema

FACT BOX

Classification

ACTIVITIES 1.1 1.2 2.1 3.1 4.1 6.2

Introduction

To understand pupils' difficulties with the process of *Classification*, you need to understand two ideas: variables and values. A *variable* is simply a way in which things vary from one another. Colour, shape, and number of legs are all variables. Each variable may have a number of values. The variable 'colour' may have the *values* blue, green, red, etc. *Classification* problems become more difficult for pupils as the number of variables increases, and as the number of values of each variable increases.

Aim

Even elementary work on living and non-living things requires them to be put into groups with some characteristics in common: that is, to be classified. *Classification* problems can be graded in difficulty according to how many variables are involved, how many values each variable has, and how clearly defined each set is within the classification.

Activity 1.1: Who am I? invites the pupils to make links between the shapes of animals and their skeletons.

Activity 1.2: All these Bones requires the pupils to classify different human bones according to various criteria, e.g. shape, function, strength.

This activity also covers *Seriation* – see the *Seriation* Schema Fact Box on page 42. The information specific to this activity for *Seriation* is: [this activity] asks pupils to consider the strength of each bone.

Activity 2.1: Where do I Live? requires the pupils to classify animals according to their native habitats

Activity 3.1: How Hot are You? requires the pupils to classify scenarios according to given temperatures and match these to the thermometers given.

Activity 4.1: Where does it Belong? invites the pupils to consider criteria for grouping various substances while thinking about solids and liquids.

Activity 6.2: Do I Work? is an activity where pupils identify those circuits that make a bulb light up.

Moving and growing **Activity 1.2**

All these Bones

Aim

Pupils are challenged to identify bones of the human body. They classify them. They consider their strength and order them from strongest to weakest. This may produce cognitive conflict as pupils will consider 'strength' from various perspectives. They begin to consider shape and strength in relation to function.

Materials

Supplied

Resource sheets 7 and 8, which are photocopiable pages, each with drawings of human bones. The bones are identified below, for your reference. ***Please note:* You should not reveal this information to the pupils in advance of the activity.**

- Resource sheet 7: 1: fibula (lower leg), 2: radius (forearm), 3: finger, 4: vertebra, 5: pelvis, 6: skull.
- Resource sheet 8: 7: toe, 8: scapula (shoulder blade), 9: ulna (forearm), 10: tibia (lower leg), 11: rib, 12: humerus (upper arm).

Not supplied

- Bones can often be borrowed from libraries. Some schools have plastic replicas: these can be useful if they are accurate representations, as they can be used later in other science lessons.
- One large sheet of paper and some Blu-Tack® for each group.

Before you start

Take photocopies of Resource sheets 7 and 8 – one of each for each group. Cut the photocopied sheets to make 12 cards per group.

Activity

Concrete preparation

- Give the pupils the pictures of the bones, and any real/replica bones, if you have them. **What animal do you think these belong to? Why? Do you think they are similar to other animals? They are human bones. Can you recognise which bones they are?** Give the pupils time to identify them. Ask them to give reasons for their choice.

Cognitive conflict and social construction: Part 1

- **Now, look at the bones and put them into groups. Think about similarities and differences. When you have finished you need to be able to explain why you have put the bones in the groups that you have chosen.** Give the groups time to discuss ways of grouping the bones and to agree reasons for their choice.

- Ask each group how they classified the bones.
- ***Class sharing:* What groups did you put the bones into? Why did you put those together?**
- **Put all the bones back into the centre and classify them in a different way. This time use only 2 groups.** Classifying in just 2 groups encourages the pupils to focus on specific criteria.
- ***Class sharing:* What groups did you choose? Why? Could you fit all the bones into these 2 groups? Which were difficult? Why?** Encourage the discussion to move towards the purpose of the bones in terms of support and protection.

Metacognition (Whole class)

This is an opportunity for pupils to consider their decisions and the processes used in making them.

- **We are going to think about the thinking we did. How did you start thinking about this task? Did you change your way of thinking? Perhaps somebody had an idea that took you in a different direction. Think about the journey of your ideas.**
- **What made this difficult? Was any bone particularly difficult? Why? What did you think about to solve the difficulty? How were you thinking? What would have helped you to do this task more easily?**
- Encourage the pupils to reflect on their thinking processes. **What were you thinking about when you made these decisions?** Encourage different group members to share the points for discussion. **Were there any bones that you were not sure about? Which caused disagreements? How did you resolve them?** Ask the pupils whether there are questions that they would like to ask the other groups. **Are there any groups that disagree with each other? If so, why?**

Cognitive conflict and social construction: Part 2

- **Your task now is to think about strength. Put the bones in order from strongest to weakest.** Give the groups time to identify and order the bones. Give the groups Blu-Tack® to attach the pictures to a large piece of paper in the order of their choice. Display these for all to see. Discuss differences and similarities in their choices. Ask them to explain why they chose that order.
- Encourage the pupils to challenge each other. **What clues helped you to decide how strong the bones are? Why do you think these bones are strong? Which bones are the strongest? What can you say about them?** They might think about similarities and differences, function and strength in relation to shape.

  Here are some examples of groupings that pupils suggest:

  - long bones
  - fat bones
  - little bones
  - bones from the top half of the body
  - bones from the lower half of the body
  - straight bones/round bones
  - stick bones/stone-like bones.

Metacognition

This is an opportunity to reflect on the thinking process. It helps pupils to realise that ideas get prioritised. They need to learn to think around various criteria in order to prioritise appropriately.

We need to think now about how thinking about this task can help us in other tasks. Think about ideas you shared. Perhaps one idea turned out to be more important than others. What kind of thinking have you been doing? How did that help you? Could you have thought about this differently? Why would that have helped? What have you learned today? How did you learn that?

Schema

FACT BOX

Concrete modelling

ACTIVITIES 1.3 4.3 6.1

Introduction

Concrete modelling is the building of simple theoretical models that offer an explanation for observations. In concrete models, each element in the model has a specific concrete referent in reality.

Aim

Experience in concrete modelling will help the pupils to understand the relationships between a number of factors or variables, all of which are amenable to immediate perception because they are 'concrete' (that is, real).

Activity 1.3: What makes me Move? invites the pupils to think about links between bones, muscles and joints and how they work in conjunction with each other.

Activity 4.3: Sorting out the Mix-ups requires pupils to think about the properties of substances and how these influence the ways in which substances can be separated.

Activity 6.1: My Bulb won't Work requires pupils to think about how a circuit works and to devise a way of explaining it to someone who does not understand.

Moving and growing **Activity 1.3**

What makes me Move?

Aim

Pupils think about how animals move by considering bones and what produces movement. They consider the different features that enable bones to move. The pupils classify parts of the body that move in similar ways. They then begin to think about how to make a model of one type of joint.

Materials

None required. You could have a selection of card, paper fasteners, old tights, elastic bands, springs, glue and scissors at the ready, but not on view. Pupils could be given the opportunity to make their model in a subsequent science or design and technology lesson.

Activity

Concrete preparation (Whole class)

- **Talk in your groups about what you know already about bones.** After about 5 minutes, ask the pupils to agree on the three most important facts about bones.
- ***Class sharing:*** Ask for one idea from each group in turn. Start with pupils who are least likely to choose to feedback.

Cognitive conflict and social construction: Part 1

- **Bones are hard and not flexible, so how can I move my arm like this?** (You bend your arm at the elbow to illustrate the point.) **Discuss this in your groups and agree how you think this happens.** Give the groups time to discuss and come up with suggestions. Tell the pupils: **You can draw a sketch if that would help you to explain.**
- ***Class sharing:*** Listen to the ideas from each group. Encourage each group to question and challenge others.

Metacognition (Whole class)

It is important for pupils to think about ideas that conflict. They need to consider carefully how to decide upon which idea to follow. They have to learn to go beyond personalities to consider the problem and use various criteria to help in resolving the challenge.

- **Let's think now about our thinking. I wonder what ideas have helped us to think better today. In what ways were you trying to solve your problem? What disagreements did you have? How did you resolve them? Could you have thought about this in a different way? How would that have helped you?**

Cognitive conflict and social construction: Part 2 (Groups)

- **Think of another part of your body that moves in a different way. Discuss how you think this part moves. Think about other parts of your body that move. Put all the ones that move in similar ways together so that you have groups. What are the differences between** [one part of your body] **and** [another part]? **What are the similarities?**
  Pupils' suggestions include:
  - elbows, knees, fingers – move like doors
  - shoulders, ankles – go roundways
  - top of leg/top of arm – move in all directions.
- **I am going to explain one way of moving to a younger class. I want to make a model of one way of moving to help them to understand. Can you design one for me? Later, you will use your design to make the model. You need to think about the materials you are going to use as well as how to make your model work.**
- ***Class sharing:*** Listen to their ideas. Tell the pupils to ask detailed questions of each other, explain what parts of the explanations they do not understand and say what they disagree with. This will encourage all the pupils to become more precise in their reasoning.

Metacognition (Whole class)

It is important to give pupils the opportunity to develop conscious awareness of their thinking processes. To help them do this, encourage the discussion.

- **Now we are going to think about the thinking that we have been doing. Thinking about our thinking helps us to be more clear about the ideas that help us. Perhaps we will be able to use those ideas in other tasks. What were we thinking about? How did you go about solving these problems today? What was really difficult? What confused you? How did the confusion clear? Can you think of anything in our everyday lives that moves in similar ways to parts of our bodies?** Pupils may think of specific toys, hinges or mechanical parts (see list above). **What kind of thinking were you using today? Where else would this help you to learn more?**

Schema

FACT BOX

Classification

ACTIVITIES 1.1 1.2 2.1 3.1 4.1 6.2

Introduction

To understand pupils' difficulties with the process of *Classification*, you need to understand two ideas: variables and values. A *variable* is simply a way in which things vary from one another. Colour, shape, and number of legs are all variables. Each variable may have a number of values. The variable 'colour' may have the *values* blue, green, red, etc. *Classification* problems become more difficult for pupils as the number of variables increases, and as the number of values of each variable increases.

Aim

Even elementary work on living and non-living things requires them to be put into groups with some characteristics in common: that is, to be classified. *Classification* problems can be graded in difficulty according to how many variables are involved, how many values each variable has, and how clearly defined each set is within the classification.

Activity 1.1: Who am I? invites the pupils to make links between the shapes of animals and their skeletons.

Activity 1.2: All these Bones requires the pupils to classify different human bones according to various criteria, e.g. shape, function, strength.

Activity 2.1: Where do I Live? requires the pupils to classify animals according to their native habitats.

Activity 3.1: How Hot are You? invites the pupils to classify scenarios according to given temperatures and match these to the thermometers given.

Activity 4.1: Where does it Belong? asks the pupils to consider criteria for grouping various substances while thinking about solids and liquids.

Activity 6.2: Do I Work? is an activity where pupils identify those circuits that make a bulb light up.

Habitats **Activity 2.1**

Where do I Live?

Aim

The pupils will be challenged to think about animals and how they are adapted to survive in their habitats.

Materials

Supplied

Resource sheets 9–11, which are photocopiable pages, each showing a set of 6 pictures of animals. The animals are identified below, for your reference. ***Please note:* You should not reveal this information to the pupils in advance of the activity**.

- Resource sheet 9: 1: squirrel, 2: heron, 3: rabbit, 4: pigeon, 5: seagull, 6: frog.
- Resource sheet 10: 7: snake, 8: worm, 9: owl, 10: kestrel, 11: snail, 12: mouse
- Resource sheet 11: 13: badger, 14: hedgehog, 15: desert rat, 16: sheep, 17: chicken; 18: fox.

Resource sheets 12 and 13, which are photocopiable pages, each showing a set of 3 different habitats, as follows:

- Resource sheet 12: 1: mountain, 2: beach, 3: lake.
- Resource sheet 13: 4: desert, 5: farmland, 6: garden.

Not supplied

- Some Blu-Tack® for each group.

Before you start

Take photocopies of Resource sheets 9–11 – one of each sheet for each group. Cut the photocopied sheets to make 18 animal cards per group. Take photocopies of Resource sheets 12 and 13 – one of each sheet for each group. Cut the photocopied sheets to make 6 habitat cards per group and stick each one in the centre of a sheet of A3 paper. Keep the animal cards and the habitat cards separate from each other.

Activity

Concrete preparation (Groups)

- Hand out the animal cards (18 per group). Tell the pupils: **Have a look at the pictures in your groups. Are there any animals that you do not recognise?** Give the pupils a few moments to talk about the pictures. Check that all can be identified. **What do you already know about these animals? Talk in your groups and share anything you know about them.** After a few minutes, ensure that all the animals can be named.

Cognitive conflict and social construction: Part 1 (Groups)

- **Now sort the animals into groups. You need to be able to explain your reasons.** Give the pupils time to classify the pictures. Encourage them to talk about various ways of classifying. Walk around the groups. Listen, so that you can choose ideas to share in the class discussion.
- ***Class sharing:*** Ask each group to explain the criteria they used to sort their pictures. Listen for their reasons. When all have shared, encourage the pupils to question and challenge each other.

Metacognition (Whole class)

- Ask the pupils to share their ideas about what helped them to do this task. **What helped you to decide which group to put animals in? What aspects made it difficult or easy? Why? Did you change your mind about any animal? Why? What kind of thinking have you been doing?**

Cognitive conflict and social construction: Part 2 (Groups)

- Give each group the pictures of habitats and ask the pupils to look at them. The challenge is to match the animals to the habitats in which they live. Allow a few moments for the pupils to discuss each habitat to ensure that they recognise it. **What do you know about these places that would be useful to this challenge?** Ask the pupils to classify each animal according to the habitat in which it lives best. The conflict comes when some animals may live in more than one. Ask the groups to Blu-Tack® the animal pictures beside the selected habitat pictures, then display them to each other: it helps the pupils who struggle with reading to see the ideas in pictorial form. When they have finished, ask them to share their ideas. Direct the discussion to how they decided which habitat was best. **Why does ... live in that habitat? What makes that habitat a good place for a ... ?** They should use words like *predator, prey, food chain ...*
- ***Class sharing:*** The pupils are sitting in their groups but attending to the whole-class discussion. Encourage them to respond to and discuss other groups' ideas; pupil contributions need not all go via the teacher. Each group shares its ideas. The discussion will centre on the differences and discrepancies in decisions made. Write the pupils' ideas on the whiteboard for all to see.

Metacognition (Whole class)

Patterns in data reflect important themes that need reflection and consideration. Pupils need opportunities to look for patterns in the natural world and reflect on what they mean.

Pupils' suggestions for groupings include:

- all birds
- all found in a forest/at the seaside/on a farm/in a garden
- fly/swim/walk.

Possible habitat groupings include the following – but, of course, very little is fixed:

- mountain – kestrel
- beach – seagull
- lake – frog, heron
- desert – snake, desert rat
- farmland – squirrel, rabbit, hedgehog, sheep, chicken, badger, fox
- garden – pigeon, worm, mouse, snail.

- **What do you notice about the choices?** Allow the class to reflect and to look for patterns, e.g. **Is there one animal that everybody has put in the same habitat? What do you think has influenced your choices?** Encourage the pupils to reflect on discussions that have influenced them.
- **What have we been thinking about? How have we thought about it? What have you learnt? How did you learn that? What helped you? Why? What made the task difficult? Why? If we had a similar task another day, what would help us from what we have discussed today?**
- Are there any questions that you want the pupils to explore on the subject of habitats? If so, display these in a prominent place so that they can be investigated throughout the topic.

Please note: **Keep the pictures, as grouped, to use in Activity 2.2: How am I Adapted?**

Schema

FACT BOX

Causality

ACTIVITIES 2.2 2.3 5.1 5.2 6.3

Introduction

Causality is a special type of relationship between variables. What causes what? The confusion of correlation (things happening together) with *Causality* (one making the other happen) is a problem that besets even otherwise intelligent adults: the link between a cause and an effect is not always obvious. Three- and four-year-olds may suggest that 'The wind is caused by the trees waving back and forth'. Although few eight- and nine-year-olds are likely to hold this belief, the relationship between different variables may still be problematic.

Aim

The pupils are asked to explore *Causality* in a variety of contexts, such as the relationship between habitat and animal characteristics, or force and the subsequent movement.

Activity 2.2: How am I Adapted? encourages the pupils to develop an understanding of the relationship between animals' characteristics and the habitats in which they live.

Activity 2.3: What am I? explores the relationship between characteristics and habitat in a game. Once the pupils have made the causal link, they are asked to use this to make predictions about unknown animals.

Activity 5.1: Where are the Forces? examines the causal relationships existing between the movement of an object/person and the forces being exerted.

Activity 5.2: Can you Change the Force? requires the pupils to explore this relationship further. They will think about which force to change and how to measure it. In the process they will discover some of the complexities of investigating forces with accuracy.

Activity 6.3: Controlling the Light requires pupils to think about the relationships between the bulb, the switch and the battery. They investigate the effects on the light when these are altered.

Habitats **Activity 2.2**

How am I Adapted?

Aim

Pupils are challenged to think about certain animals and identify particular characteristics that enable them to live in specified habitats. They think about particular adaptations that make it possible for them to live where they do.

Materials

Supplied

- Resource sheet 14, which is a photocopiable picture of a camel.
- The animal and habitat pictures (taken from Resource sheets 9–13), as grouped by the pupils in **Activity 2.1: Where do I Live?**

Before you start

Take photocopies of Resource sheet 14 – one for each group.

Activity

Concrete preparation (Groups)

Give each group the picture of a camel. Ask them to think about where a camel lives and to identify any characteristic that enables this animal to live in this habitat.

List the ideas that the groups suggest. Are there any that another group disagrees with? They should be thinking about:

- the hump – stores fluid for use when there is none available to drink;
- long eye-lashes – arranged in two rows, for protection against blowing sand;
- broad feet – these have thick skin under the soles to protect camels from the burning desert sand;
- diet – in tough conditions the camel is able to live on very little food. It has very strong, rubbery lips that allow it to eat thorns. (It also has a four-chambered stomach and a strong digestive system.)

Cognitive conflict and social construction: Part 1 (Groups)

- Give each group the set of pictures of habitats and animals as they sorted them in the last activity. **What do you know already that will help you?** Ask them to identify as many aspects as they can that help each animal to live in the habitat.

Remind them they will have to explain their reasons to the class. When most groups are ready, ask them to think of another habitat of which they do not have a picture (e.g. a town, the Arctic, a river and riverbank). Ask them to think of at least one animal that is adapted to live in this habitat.

- ***Class sharing:*** When the groups are ready, ask them to share their ideas. Take each habitat in turn and then take each group's chosen animal. Encourage the addition of new ideas rather than repeating ones that have already been given. It is very important that each group gets a chance to go first. In this way, each group contributes the original ideas and all groups have to listen to each other carefully to decide which of their ideas have not yet been shared by others. The discussion of animals' adaptations to their habitat should encompass: parts of the body (e.g. feet/wings/fins), colour, diet, mating, rearing the young and protection.

Metacognition (Whole class)

It is important to take this time to consider what has been learnt so far. This encourages pupils to use this learning during the later part of the lesson and beyond.

- **We have been thinking about many ideas. Some ideas are more useful for some tasks than others. Talking about the ideas we have may give other groups ideas that they can use next time. What kind of thinking have we been doing? What helped you? What made it difficult? What could help you to learn more about this? What is it like when we add to each others' ideas? Is that helpful? Why? Why not?**

Cognitive conflict and social construction: Part 2 (Groups)

- **Several groups have mentioned food as important. Much of that food consists of plants. How do the plants survive in these habitats? What happens when the food does not survive? What happens when a habitat is reduced or disappears? What causes these dangers?** Ask the groups to choose one habitat and think about dangers within that habitat. It is beneficial if the class can agree that each group will think about a different habitat. In this way knowledge will be extended. Also, the others will have more questions to ask about habitats they have not had time to consider. **What effects do these dangers have on all that live here? What are the results if these dangers go to extremes?**
- ***Class sharing:*** Ask each group to share their ideas. Other groups can take a few minutes after each sharing to discuss a question they could ask that would provide further information. If the group does not know the answers, they can note the question for further investigation.

Metacognition (Whole class)

- Spend some time encouraging the pupils to think about the ideas they have been sharing. Verbalising this thinking will help them to evaluate it. They should be realising that this conscious reflection on their thinking is helping to make the thinking more accessible in other tasks.
- **What have you been thinking about? How have you been thinking about it? Would any other kind of thinking help you? What made this difficult? How could we overcome these difficulties? If you wanted to explain the main points that you have learnt, what would you say?**
- Make a list of questions that need time for investigation.

Schema

FACT BOX

Causality

ACTIVITIES 2.2 2.3 5.1 5.2 6.3

Introduction

Causality is a special type of relationship between variables. What causes what? The confusion of correlation (things happening together) with *Causality* (one making the other happen) is a problem that besets even otherwise intelligent adults: the link between a cause and an effect is not always obvious. Three- and four-year-olds may suggest that 'The wind is caused by the trees waving back and forth'. Although few eight- and nine-year-olds are likely to hold this belief, the relationship between different variables may still be problematic.

Aim

The pupils are asked to explore *Causality* in a variety of contexts, such as the relationship between habitat and animal characteristics, or force and the subsequent movement.

Activity 2.2: How am I Adapted? encourages the pupils to develop an understanding of the relationship between animals' characteristics and the habitats in which they live.

Activity 2.3: What am I? explores the relationship between characteristics and habitat in a game. Once the pupils have made the causal link, they are asked to use this to make predictions about unknown animals.

Activity 5.1: Where are the Forces? examines the causal relationships existing between the movement of an object/person and the forces being exerted.

Activity 5.2: Can you Change the Force? requires the pupils to explore this relationship further. They will think about which force to change and how to measure it. In the process they will discover some of the complexities of investigating forces with accuracy.

Activity 6.3: Controlling the Light requires pupils to think about the relationships between the bulb, the switch and the battery. They investigate the effects on the light when these are altered.

Habitats **Activity 2.3**

What am I?

Aim

This activity will challenge pupils to think about where animals live and how they may have to adapt if their habitat is threatened. Listening to pupils' ideas will give an indication of how much has been learnt during previous weeks. This is a good opportunity for the teacher to make formative assessments.

Materials

None required.

Activity

Concrete preparation (Whole class)

- Ask the pupils to listen and work out which habitat this animal lives in. **I have four legs. My back legs are long and strong. I have a pale underside to my body. I eat insects and other small animals. I have a long tongue and a wide mouth. My young must live in water. I breathe through lungs and my skin. Some of my predators are herons, foxes and hedgehogs.**
- Talk together for a few minutes. Work out which animal this is and where it lives. (It is the frog, which lives around ponds and rivers in Britain.) Listen to their ideas. Discuss the clues. **Which clues made it easy? Which did not help?**

Cognitive conflict and social construction: Part 1 (Groups)

- Tell the pupils: **In your groups, think of another animal. Decide on some pieces of information to give us to help us work out where this animal lives. Some clues make the puzzle too easy and some do not help, so think carefully about what clues you really want to give.** Give the groups time to think through some of the issues before deciding on the animal. Once they have decided, encourage them to stay with that animal and to think about the areas of information they need to give, i.e. features, feeding, young, predators.
- ***Class sharing:*** When the groups have had enough time, they take it in turns to give their clues. One pupil within each group can give each clue so that they are all involved. When the other pupils suggest an animal as a response, they need to give a reason, e.g. *I think it could be a frog because their young are tadpoles and need to live in water. Also, frogs eat small animals.*

Metacognition (Whole class)

- Encourage the pupils to reflect on the thinking they have been engaged in. This is important because pupils need to learn to prioritise ideas that are crucial above those which are supplementary and less important. Some ideas may even distract or detract from what is relevant. **What was difficult about this activity? Was it easier to choose clues or to work out another group's ideas? What clues helped you most? Which made it too easy? Why? Which did not help? Why? What have you learnt that you think might help you with other tasks? Why? Did you change your mind about anything? What helped you to do this?**

Cognitive conflict and social construction: Part 2

- **A frog can live on land *near water* and also *in water*. It can live in a varied habitat. When habitats are threatened, animals have to adapt to different habitats so their species survives. This takes a long period of time – hundreds of years. But we are going to imagine that we can speed things up. We are going to imagine an animal in one habitat. Something threatens its habitat. You need to decide what the problem is and what it needs to do about it. Where is it going to go and live? What adaptations will it need to make in order to survive? How will it change? Will it change its diet, places of shelter, ways of mating, how it looks after its young? The main idea it has is that it does not want to become extinct. You can present your ideas as you like.**
- ***Class sharing:*** Each group presents its ideas while the others listen. It is important that they express their reasons, e.g. *It has to change its diet and start eating different plants. This means that its teeth have to change shape because …*
- When each group has finished, invite other groups to ask them questions and challenge them on ideas that may not be clear or may be flawed in some way. (This activity can be extended into English [persuasive writing] and art, if appropriate.)

Metacognition (Whole class)

Leaving time at the end of the activity is very important. This conscious reflection helps pupils to become more aware of the sort of thinking that helps them. It also encourages them to evaluate the thinking they did not use or discarded as unhelpful for this task. After this activity, ask: **What were you thinking about as you were doing the task? What kind of thinking were you using? What made this difficult? What did you need that helped you? What have you learnt about doing a task like this that would help you in future? Does thinking about these sorts of ideas give you any thoughts about our job in looking after habitats? How could we use this learning? How difficult was it to present your ideas? Which ideas did you find difficult to understand? What was making this difficult?**

The last three questions represent an important piece of clarification. Recognising what is difficult to understand when listening to someone else's presentation helps pupils to understand how important clarity of expression is to the listener's understanding.

Schema

FACT BOX

Classification

ACTIVITIES 1.1 1.2 2.1 3.1 4.1 6.2

Introduction

To understand pupils' difficulties with the process of *Classification*, you need to understand two ideas: variables and values. A *variable* is simply a way in which things vary from one another. Colour, shape, and number of legs are all variables. Each variable may have a number of values. The variable 'colour' may have the *values* blue, green, red, etc. *Classification* problems become more difficult for pupils as the number of variables increases, and as the number of values of each variable increases.

Aim

Even elementary work on living and non-living things requires them to be put into groups with some characteristics in common: that is, to be classified. *Classification* problems can be graded in difficulty according to how many variables are involved, how many values each variable has, and how clearly defined each set is within the classification.

Activity 1.1: Who am I? invites the pupils to make links between the shapes of animals and their skeletons.

Activity 1.2: All these Bones requires the pupils to classify different human bones according to various criteria, e.g. shape, function, strength.

Activity 2.1: Where do I Live? requires the pupils to classify animals according to their native habitats.

Activity 3.1: How Hot are You? invites the pupils to classify scenarios according to given temperatures and match these to the thermometers given.

Activity 4.1: Where does it Belong? asks the pupils to consider criteria for grouping various substances while thinking about solids and liquids.

Activity 6.2: Do I Work? is an activity where pupils identify those circuits that make a bulb light up.

Keeping warm **Activity 3.1**

How Hot are You?

Aim

The pupils are asked to think about the temperatures of some ordinary items. They will be expected to come to a final group decision, which will encourage them to provide justifications for their choices. Most justifications will challenge the pupils to think about temperatures and the measurement of temperature on thermometers.

Materials

Supplied

- Resource sheet 15, which is an A3 photocopiable sheet (bound into the back of this book) showing an enlarged picture of a thermometer.
- Resource sheets 16 and 17, which are photocopiable sheets, each showing pictures of 6 thermometers. The first 4 thermometers (Resource sheet 16) are labelled A; the remaining 8 (Resource sheets 16 and 17) are labelled B. All 12 thermometers show different temperatures.
- Resource sheet 18, which is a photocopiable sheet describing 12 separate scenarios: 4 of these are labelled A, and 8 are labelled B.

Not supplied

- For each group, a large sheet of paper and some glue.

Before you start

Take one A3 photocopy of Resource sheet 15, to display to the class.

Take photocopies of Resource sheets 16 and 17 – one for each group. Cut the photocopied sheets to make 12 thermometer cards per group. The thermometer cards labelled A are used for *Cognitive conflict and social construction: Part 1* and those labelled B are for *Part 2*.

You may also wish to make an OHT of Resource sheets 16 and 17, or enlarge them to display on the whiteboard when you discuss how pupils have matched the temperatures on the thermometers with the different scenarios described.

Take photocopies of Resource sheet 18 – one for each group. Cut the photocopied sheets to make 12 scenario cards per group. The scenario cards labelled A are used for *Cognitive conflict and social construction: Part 1* and those labelled B are for *Part 2*.

Activity

Concrete preparation

- Show the class your photocopy of Resource sheet 15 – showing an enlarged thermometer. Ask the pupils: **What can you tell me about this? What do you know about thermometers? What does a thermometer measure? How does it work?**
- Give each group the 4 thermometer cards labelled A, which you have photocopied from Resource sheet 16. Keep the cards labelled B for later use. Tell the pupils: **Have a look at the thermometers in your group. What do you notice about them? What do you think thermometers measure?** Ask the pupils to talk about the thermometers. After 2 minutes, ask: **Can you tell me what your group said?**

Cognitive conflict and social construction: Part 1

- Give each group the scenario cards labelled A, which you have photocopied from Resource sheet 18 (left-hand column). Keep the cards labelled B for use later. Tell the pupils: **I want you to talk about the cards. Do you recognise these situations? What temperatures could these be?** Give the pupils a few minutes for discussion. Encourage whole-class discussion on the more difficult ones (e.g. temperature of a healthy person).
- Ask the pupils to look again at the temperature cards labelled A. **I want you to match up the scenarios with the temperature that you think each one is. Place the thermometer and the scenario card that you think matches alongside one another.** Move around the groups. Make a mental note of any interesting conversations to share with the class. Stop the class after about 10 minutes.
- ***Class sharing:*** Choose a spokesperson from each group to tell you about the group's decisions. **Which temperature did you choose for the boiling water?** Write the responses where the whole class can see them: e.g., you could write each one next to the thermometer showing the appropriate temperature on your OHT of Resource sheet 16, or on the enlarged copy you have made to display on the whiteboard.
- Ask each group to explain the criteria they used to match their pictures. **Why did you put those 2 together? What is causing the temperature rise there? I was wondering if that one could match with this one? What do you think?** Record each group's ideas. When all the groups have given their responses, discuss reasons for each choice. Discuss any discrepancies. When they have all shared, encourage the pupils to question and challenge each other if they disagree. If there are no discrepancies, say what *you* thought, making your ideas different from theirs. This will challenge them to think carefully about their reasons. Give the groups a few minutes to discuss whether they want to change their minds. Repeat this for each of the 4 scenarios.
- The correct matches of scenarios and temperatures are as follows:

• a healthy person	37°C	(A1)
• boiling water	100°C	(A4)
• an ice cube	0°C	(A3)
• the classroom at midday in December	17°C	(A2)

Metacognition

Challenge pupils to say how they arrived at their decisions. Each group may want to challenge another group's ideas. One issue that causes much discussion is the temperature of a healthy person. Ask: **What made you decide on the temperature of a healthy person? What experiences have you had to suggest this? What do you notice about your choices? Can you remember what you were talking and thinking about when you were choosing the temperatures? Which scenario was the hardest for you to decide on? Why?**

You may want to give the groups a few minutes to reflect on this, before asking them to share what they remember. **Did any other groups have a similar problem? What helped you to decide**

which thermometer to put with each scenario? What aspects made it difficult? Why? Was there a point when you changed your mind? Why did this happen? What had you learnt before that helped you to do this task or made it more difficult? Invite pupils from all groups to comment and discuss.

Cognitive conflict and social construction: Part 2

- Ask the groups to put the cards to one side. Give each group the scenario cards labelled B, which you photocopied from Resource sheet 18, and the thermometer cards labelled B, which you photocopied from Resource sheets 16 and 17. Tell the pupils: **You are going to match up more temperatures now.** These may be more difficult and may cause more discussion. Encourage the pupils to discuss possibilities before they finally decide. Give the groups about 10 minutes to discuss this challenge. As before, move around the groups, listening for interesting conversations. **What are your choices?**
- ***Class sharing:*** Give each group time to explain what they think and to give their reasons. Take one card at a time and discuss any differences so that a class agreement can be reached.
- The correct matches of scenarios and temperatures are as follows:

• a person with 'flu	41°C	(B7)
• a glass of water just taken from the tap	9°C	(B1)
• a garden pond at midday in July	20°C	(B8)
• a garden in Spain at midday in August	32°C	(B4)
• a glass of lemonade just poured from a bottle in the fridge	2.5°C	(B2)
• the classroom at midday in September	16°C	(B5)
• the classroom at midday in July	25°C	(B6)
• playing in the snow at midday in the winter	1°C	(B3)

Metacognition (Whole class)

You will have noticed which temperatures have caused the pupils the most discussion and the most difficulty. Focus on those situations. Note that the temperature in the classroom in September (16°C) is lower than that in December (17°C) because of the effects of central heating during the winter months. Try to establish what they thought at the beginning and what led them to change their minds. Then be clear about what they think at the end of the activity. **What have you been thinking about? What kind of thinking have you been doing? What have you learnt? How did you learn that? What helped you to learn this? Why? What made the task difficult? Why? What have you learned today that you think could be useful in another activity? If we were going to teach Year 2 (P3) about recording their ideas, what advice would we give them?**

Encourage the pupils to recognise that sometimes we hold ideas in our minds that are not quite accurate. **As we learn, we change our ideas and we also develop new ideas.** Ask the pupils to glue the thermometer cards onto a large sheet of paper, next to the relevant scenario cards.

Remind the pupils: **Thermometers measure temperature. Are there any questions that you want to ask that we could explore later during this topic?** Display these in a prominent place in the classroom.

> ***Please note:* Keep the large sheets of paper, on which the pupils have glued the thermometer and scenario cards, to use as the starter for Activity 3.2: Hotter or Colder? – when the pupils will need to be able to identify their group response.**
>
> **These can be displayed in the classroom. Hopefully, some ideas may develop and pupils may enter into discussions with each other about these ideas. In this way, the learning continues as they scaffold ideas for each other.**

Schema

FACT BOX

Relationship between variables

ACTIVITY 3.2 5.3

Introduction

'The stronger the wind, the faster I can walk to school.' Is that true? In other words, is there a relationship between the variable 'strength of wind' and the variable 'how fast one can walk'? Science is all about exploring relationships between variables and two activities in this programme give pupils an opportunity to do just that.

Aim

The pupils are encouraged to identify and consider the relationships between different events or processes. It is not just a case of *whether* things 'go together' but *how* they go together: as one goes up, does the other go up too, or go down, or isn't it connected at all?

Activity 3.2: Hotter or Colder? requires the pupils to consider changes in temperature over a period of time.

Activity 5.3: Late for School invites pupils to consider the effect of the wind on the speed at which they can walk.

Keeping warm Activity 3.2

Hotter or Colder?

Aim

Pupils will use the charts created in the last activity. They will then decide what happens to the temperatures after a period of 4 hours and discuss the causes of changes in temperatures.

Materials

Supplied

- Resource sheet 19, which is a photocopiable sheet showing pictures of 6 thermometers. None of the thermometers show any temperature.

Not supplied

- Black pens to mark the temperature on each thermometer.
- Some glue, coloured pens, paper and graph paper for each group (if desired).

Before you start

Take photocopies of Resource sheet 19 – 2 copies for each group. Cut these to make a total of 12 separate cards per group.

Find the large sheets of paper on which the children glued the thermometer cards next to the relevant scenario cards during **Activity 3.1: How Hot are You?**

Activity

Concrete preparation

- Refer to the work completed in **Activity 3.1: How Hot are You?** Give each group their sheet put together during this activity. Ask the pupils to look at their sheet in their group. **What do you remember about the activity? What did you learn? How has it helped you with other work related to this topic? Have you changed your minds about anything?**

Cognitive conflict and social construction: Part 1

- **If we had the real objects/people in these different scenarios, and if each one stayed in the same position for 4 hours, what differences would be showing on the thermometers? Talk in your groups about your ideas. When you agree, you need to record your idea on the new thermometers. You will show your ideas to the class so we all need to be able to see the record.** Ask the pupils to fill in the temperatures on the blank thermometers, and glue each card onto the original sheets beside the relevant scenario.

- One possible solution showing the temperatures four hours later is given below:

A

• healthy person	37°C
• boiling water	17°C
• an ice cube	17°C
• the classroom at midday in December	13°C

B

• a person with 'flu	41°C
• a glass of water just taken from the tap	17°C
• a garden pond at midday in June	16°C
• a garden in Spain at midday in August	29°C
• a glass of lemonade just poured from a bottle in the fridge	17°C
• the classroom at midday in September	14°C
• the classroom at midday in July	20°C
• playing in the snow at midday in the winter	–2°C

- ***Class sharing:*** When the pupils have finished, ask them to share their ideas. Discuss how they decided on the differences in temperature. When each group has shared, allow time for them to challenge each other. **Why does that thermometer now show … ? What has happened to make this one change?** Pupils need to be able to discuss the difference between the temperatures and what causes the difference or what causes the temperature to remain the same.

Metacognition

Help the pupils to become more aware of the issues that they had to consider. Encourage them to think about the ideas they took on board and those they rejected. A discussion about room temperature may usefully take place. Pupils may also consider the effects of central heating. **What kind of thinking have you been doing? How did you decide what was going to happen over time? What did you have to think about before you could decide? What helped you? What made it difficult? What have you learnt about your thinking?** Encourage class discussion.

Cognitive conflict and social construction: Part 2

- Have on view some coloured pens, pencils, graph paper and squared paper of various sizes.
- **Now, in your groups, I want you to agree a method of recording each temperature 'before' and 'after', to show what is happening. You need to do this *without* just showing the thermometers *as they are* so that you can show *what has happened.***
- ***Class sharing:*** After 5 minutes, initiate a discussion about different ways of recording. The pupils need to explain what materials they need and what recording method they intend to use. This may help the groups to make a better attempt at the challenge.
- As a group, they then take the equipment required and record the initial and the final temperatures for each item. They could show the relationship between the change and the time taken.
- When the groups have had enough time, each shares its ideas. The class discusses each method proposed. **Which record is easiest to understand? Why? Which is most difficult to understand? What key things do we need to think about when recording our ideas?** Some groups may have used different colours on the thermometers and annotated them, others may have drawn graphs (such as those shown on pages 40 and 41). The pupils need to think about a systematic method that shows at a glance the temperature at the two times of measurement.

Metacognition

Encourage the pupils to consider what they have learnt. They need to become clear as to how their thinking together helped them to develop their individual ideas. **How did you come up with your**

idea? What did you have to think about and agree? What caused disagreement? How did you solve that problem? What kind of thinking were you doing? How would this help you in another task? What would you do differently next time if you had to do something like this again? Encourage the other groups to listen to the ideas and to ask the feedback group questions.

Pupils may have drawn graphs such as those shown below as part of this activity.

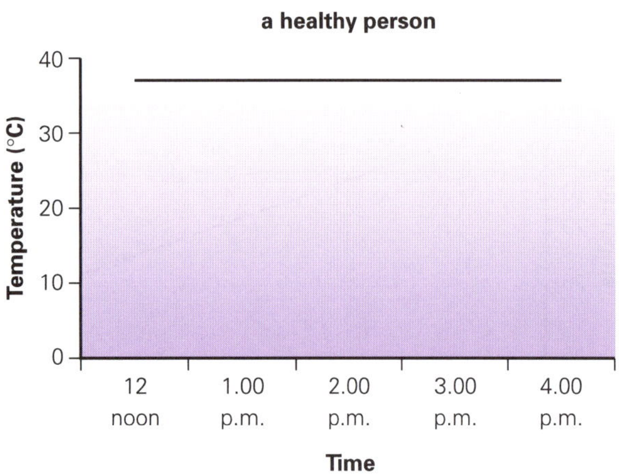

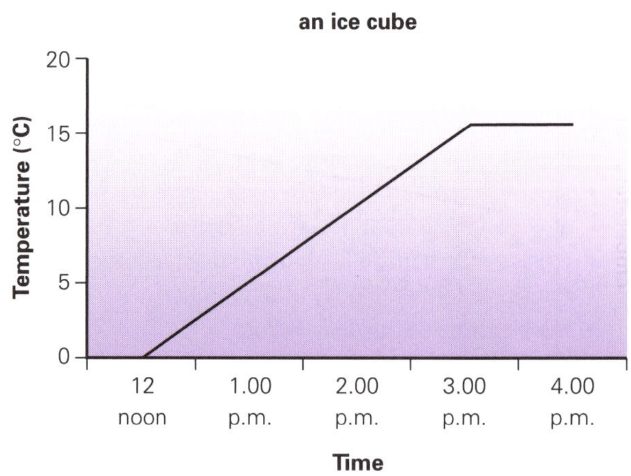

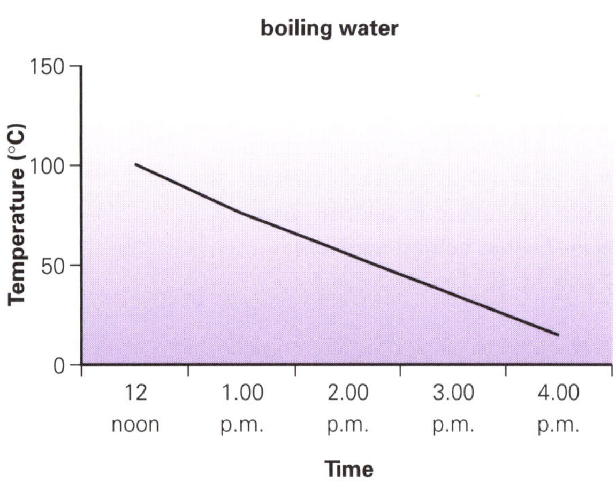

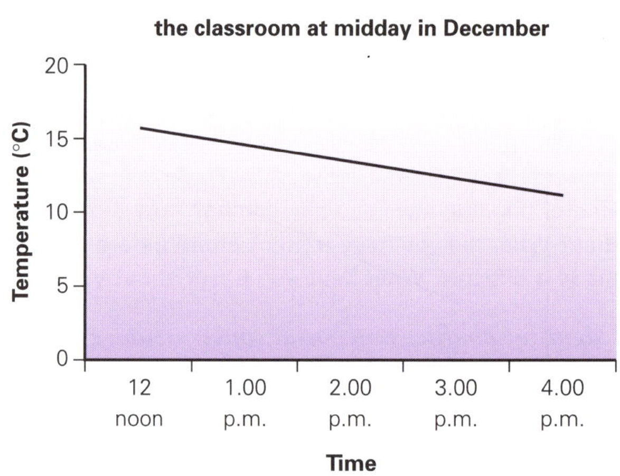

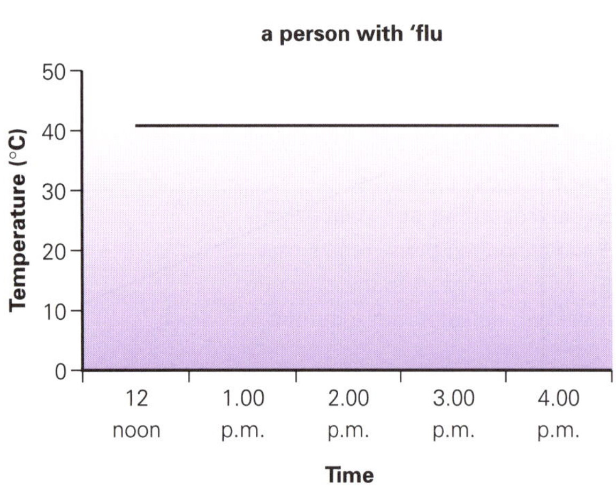

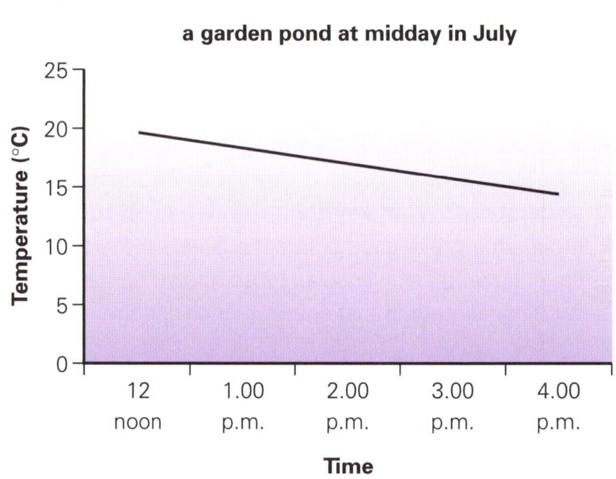

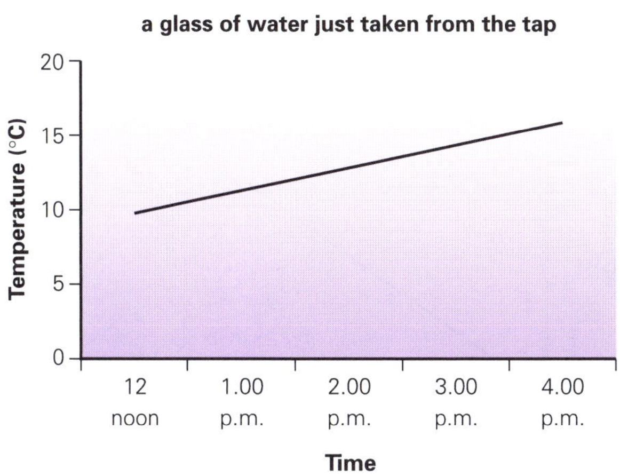
a glass of water just taken from the tap
Temperature (°C)
20
15
10
5
0
12 noon
1.00 p.m.
2.00 p.m.
3.00 p.m.
4.00 p.m.
Time

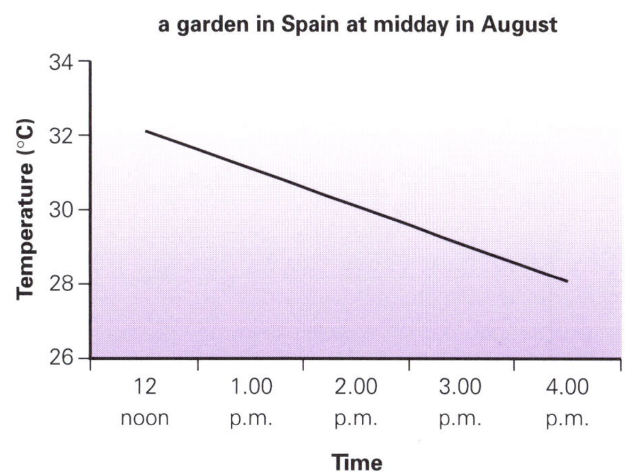
a garden in Spain at midday in August
Temperature (°C)
34
32
30
28
26
12 noon
1.00 p.m.
2.00 p.m.
3.00 p.m.
4.00 p.m.
Time

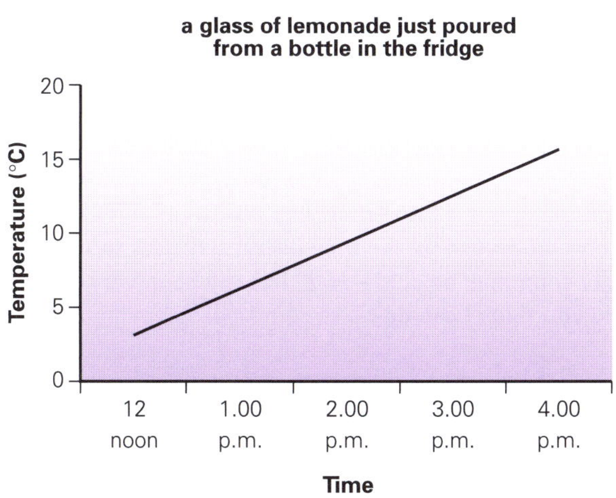
a glass of lemonade just poured from a bottle in the fridge
Temperature (°C)
20
15
10
5
0
12 noon
1.00 p.m.
2.00 p.m.
3.00 p.m.
4.00 p.m.
Time

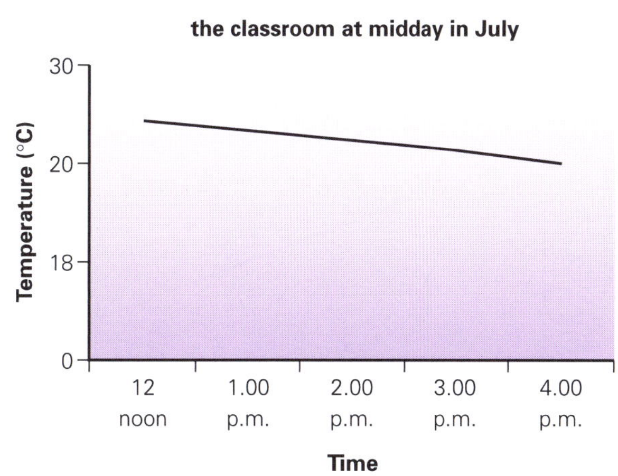
the classroom at midday in July
Temperature (°C)
30
20
18
0
12 noon
1.00 p.m.
2.00 p.m.
3.00 p.m.
4.00 p.m.
Time

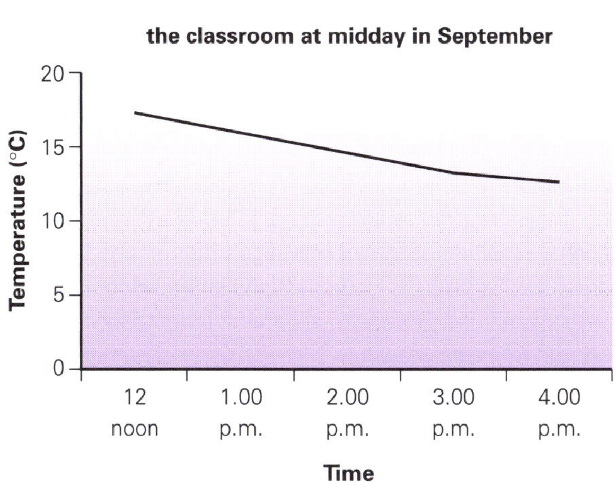
the classroom at midday in September
Temperature (°C)
20
15
10
5
0
12 noon
1.00 p.m.
2.00 p.m.
3.00 p.m.
4.00 p.m.
Time

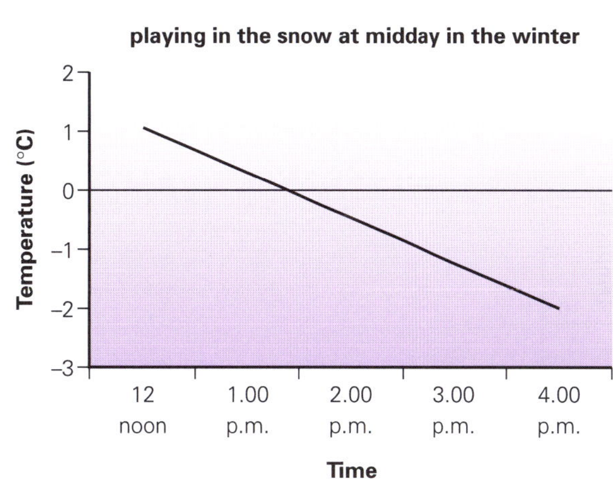
playing in the snow at midday in the winter
Temperature (°C)
2
1
0
−1
−2
−3
12 noon
1.00 p.m.
2.00 p.m.
3.00 p.m.
4.00 p.m.
Time

Schema

FACT BOX

Seriation

ACTIVITIES 1.2 3.3

Introduction

Seriation (putting things in order to form a series) is fundamental to understanding number and to many practical operations that older pupils take for granted.

Aim

The activities aim to help develop pupils' working memory capacity, as they learn to attend to several items at one time and to see how they relate to one another.

Activity 1.2: All these Bones requires pupils to consider the strength of bones and order them accordingly. This activity also covers *Classification* – see the *Classification* Schema Fact Box on page 20.

Activity 3.3: I like my Soup Hot requires pupils to consider the best material from which to make a soup bowl.

Keeping warm **Activity 3.3**

I like my Soup Hot

Aim

The pupils are asked to think about the material that would best keep some soup hot. They will need to think about how they could investigate this problem to find out.

Materials

None required.

Health and safety

No hot substances are handled during this activity, but you could nevertheless remind the pupils to be careful with hot substances, which can cause burns.

Activity

Concrete preparation

- **I am going to make a pot of soup to have for supper. I am going to invite some friends. I want to heat the soup until it boils and then pour it into bowls and put them on the table. I am worried because by the time everybody gets to the table, the soup may be cold – and I like my soup very hot. What do you think I can do?** Take some ideas from around the room.

Cognitive conflict and social construction: Part 1

- **In your groups, I want you to discuss the best ways to help me to serve hot soup. What would you do? What would you put the soup into? What would the soup be like if everybody took 5 minutes to be ready? What would it be like if my visitors took 10 minutes? … 15 minutes … 30 minutes to be ready?** Give the groups time to talk about what container would be best to use. Encourage them to explain their ideas within the group. **What material is that made from? Why do you think that would be best?**
- ***Class sharing:*** When the groups are ready, ask each one to share how they are going to solve the problem. Record their suggestions on the whiteboard. Encourage other groups to question and challenge by asking questions and making alternative suggestions. Hopefully, several different suggestions will be offered from the groups.

Metacognition

Pupils may find this difficult if they are not familiar with the properties of various materials. For them to recognise the sort of knowledge they need is useful. **What was difficult? What could you do to solve this problem? What made you think this? What were you thinking about? Was this the best way? Why? Is there another way to think about this? What helped you to come to a solution? What made it difficult? What would you need to help you further?**

Cognitive conflict and social construction: Part 2

- **How are we going to find out which is best? In your groups, discuss how we could find out which suggestion will give me the hottest soup. We have had some suggestions** [say how many] **for what material to use for the bowls. Now we need to plan this investigation.** Encourage the pupils to put the suggestions in order, starting with the one that will keep the soup hottest for longest and continuing to the one that will let the soup get coldest.
- ***Class sharing:*** When the groups have had enough time, ask them to share their ideas. They can show any diagrams or recording of ideas they have made. Encourage the other groups to challenge and question each other so as to refine their ideas.

Metacognition

Encourage pupils to briefly describe the processes they have engaged in during this activity. They may want to challenge some of the ideas. Encourage this. Also encourage discussion about why this kind of challenge helps them to develop their thinking further. **What did you need to think about? What made this difficult? What helped? Did anybody change your mind about any aspect of this work? How did that happen? What did you learn? If you were going to do anything like this again, what would you do differently? What part of your investigation will be the most difficult to do in the classroom? Why? What advice can you give us before we do these investigations?** This is important for pupils to consider so that they learn to take planning and preparation of an investigation seriously. They also need to think about how they are going to measure the results so that they can explain what they learn through conducting the investigation.

These investigations can be carried out during the next science lesson.

Schema
FACT BOX

Classification

ACTIVITIES 1.1 1.2 2.1 3.1 4.1 6.2

Introduction

To understand pupils' difficulties with the process of *Classification*, you need to understand two ideas: variables and values. A *variable* is simply a way in which things vary from one another. Colour, shape and number of legs are all variables. Each variable may have a number of values. The variable 'colour' may have the *values* blue, green, red, etc. *Classification* problems become more difficult for pupils as the number of variables increases, and as the number of values of each variable increases.

Aim

Even elementary work on living and non-living things requires them to be put into groups with some characteristics in common: that is, to be classified. *Classification* problems can be graded in difficulty according to how many variables are involved, how many values each variable has, and how clearly defined each set is within the classification.

Activity 1.1: Who am I? invites the pupils to make links between the shapes of animals and their skeletons.

Activity 1.2: All these Bones requires the pupils to classify different human bones according to various criteria, e.g. shape, function, strength.

Activity 2.1: Where do I Live? requires the pupils to classify animals according to their native habitats.

Activity 3.1: How Hot are You? requires the pupils to classify scenarios according to given temperatures and match these to the thermometers given.

Activity 4.1: Where does it Belong? invites the pupils to consider criteria for grouping various substances with an emphasis on solids and liquids.

Activity 6.2: Do I Work? is an activity where pupils identify circuits that make a bulb light up.

Solids and liquids **Activity 4.1**

Where does it Belong?

Materials

Supplied

- Resource sheets 20 and 21: 2 photocopiable pages of cards, each page labelled with the names of 12 different substances.

Before you start

Take photocopies of Resource sheets 20 and 21 – one for each group. Cut each photocopied sheet to make 12 substance cards. Place a full set of 24 cards on each group's table.

You may also want to make OHTs of the 2 resource sheets, and then cut them up for use in *Cognitive conflict and social construction: Part 2.*

Activity

Concrete preparation

- Encourage pupils to think about the materials presented to them on the cards and sort them into various groups. Eventually they will sort the materials according to whether they are solids or liquids. **Do you know what each of these substances is?** Give pupils the opportunity to explain what the least common substances are, i.e. plaster of Paris, lard.

Cognitive conflict and social construction: Part 1

- Ask the pupils to put these cards into groups. They will need to agree reasons for their choices. Pupils work together in their groups to classify the cards.
- ***Class sharing:*** **What groups did you choose? Why did you choose to put those together?**
- **Put all the cards back into the centre and classify them in a different way. If you used 2 groups this time, use 3 or 4 groups to re-classify. If you used 3 or 4 groups this time, re-classify into 2 groups.** Encourage the pupils to discuss similarities and differences between the items. Encourage them to think of different criteria. **What do you think is the same about these? What differences do you think there are?** If pupils have used solids and liquids as categories, there may be some assumptions to challenge, raising questions and some curiosity, e.g. **Your group put jelly in the 'solids' column, and this group put it in the 'liquids' column? Or: You put lard in the 'solids' column *and* you put it in the 'liquids' column. Can you both be right?**

Metacognition (Whole class)

Encourage the pupils to explain some of the ideas they discussed – some that caused disagreement, some that they could not resolve. Ask if anybody changed their mind about anything. **What enabled you to do this? What did you have to think about before you could decide what groups to put the cards into? What was difficult about this task? What helped you to do this? Is there anything you have learnt from this that you think you could use in another task? Is there anything you need to know before we go any further?**

Cognitive conflict and social construction: Part 2

- The next challenge depends upon what happened in the first part of the activity. If pupils have not used solids and liquids as criteria, this needs to be addressed. Take a set of cards. Sort them into 2 groups using solids/liquids as the criterion. Display these 2 groups on a whiteboard or flipchart, or write them on an OHT. If you have made OHTs of the 2 resource sheets, cut them up and group them on the OHP. Ask the pupils to work out, in their groups, what they think your idea for grouping is.
- If pupils used the criterion of solids/liquids in the first part of the activity, use their ideas to start this second part of the activity. **Some of these items are causing us problems and we are not sure whether they are solid or liquid. Now we need to discuss these problems and come up with a rule for deciding whether something is a solid or a liquid.**
- Pupils work in their groups until they can explain their rules for how to decide whether something is solid or liquid. When they have finished, listen to their ideas. Encourage the class to discuss these ideas, challenge each other and ask each other questions.

Metacognition (Whole class)

Encourage pupils to think about their thought processes. Challenge them to explain the thinking that helped them best. Which ideas did they reject? **What made this difficult? Was any item particularly difficult? Why was this? What did you think about to solve the difficulty? What would have helped you to do this task more easily?**

Ask pupils to list their final groups so that they can be used in the next thinking activity. Finish by asking the pupils to record 5 questions in their groups. **Ask 5 questions that you think we could use during this topic to increase our learning.** Display these questions in a visible place for use in the next activity.

Please note: **Keep the photocopies of Resource sheets 20 and 21 for use in Activity 4.2: I can't find the Sugar and Activity 4.3: Sorting out the Mix-ups.**

Schema

FACT BOX

Conservation

ACTIVITY 4.2

Introduction

Conservation is the schema that allows us to perceive that the total amount of a substance, such as water or plasticene, does not alter as it is transformed in shape: the amount is conserved.

Aim

The fact that a quantity of water remains the same when you pour it from one container to another seems pretty obvious to us, but it is not at all certain for many eight-year-olds. The aim of this activity is to help pupils to develop a schema of *Conservation*, so that the pupils understand that the *amount* of many substances stays the same, even when their *shape* or *place* has been changed.

Activity 4.2: I can't find the Sugar requires pupils to develop a simple method of separating materials one from the other.

Solids and liquids **Activity 4.2**

I can't find the Sugar

Aim

The pupils have to think about the characteristics and properties of the materials in water and find ways of separating them.

Materials

Supplied

- Resource sheets 20 and 21: 2 photocopiable pages of cards, each page labelled with the names of 12 different substances (as **Activity 4.1: Where does it Belong?**).

Not supplied

- One jug of water.

Before you start

Look out the cards you used in **Activity 4.1: Where does it Belong?** or take photocopies of Resource sheets 20 and 21 – one for each group – and cut each photocopied sheet to make 12 substance cards.

Place a full set of 24 cards on each group's table.

Activity

Concrete preparation (Groups)

- **Look at what you have on your table. Can you remember what you did with the cards in the last activity?** Ask the groups to talk about this, keeping your introduction brief. After a few minutes, stop the pupils and ask some groups to share their ideas. The purpose of this is to remind pupils of some of the properties of the materials and to allow them time to enter into discussion about them again. **Did you learn anything new last time? Are you still thinking about any of the ideas that came up?**

Cognitive conflict and social construction: Part 1 (Groups)

- Now, show the class a jug of water. **If you had the items on the cards *and* a jug of water, what groupings would you choose?** The groups discuss what happens when water is added to each of these items. They then group the materials according to their chosen criteria.

- ***Class sharing:*** The pupils sit in their groups, but in a position where they can see as many other pupils as possible. Give each group the opportunity to discuss what they think. Ask them to share what they think. Ask them to give reasons for their choices. Discuss any differences and similarities in their choices. Encourage the groups to challenge and question each other. **We don't think that goes there because ... Why do you think ... ?** If pupils use words like *melt, dissolve, solution,* write them on the whiteboard and challenge pupils to explain them. **Melt ... I'm wondering what that means?** They may say that some substances 'disappear', e.g. sugar. Challenge this by encouraging them to consider what they mean. **Has it disappeared from sight? Yes – but not in reality. Where is it? Does it still exist? What space is it taking up?** In this way, you have the opportunity to formatively assess the pupils' understanding and this will inform the teaching that is needed in subsequent activities.

Metacognition

When you were sorting the materials, how did you decide where to put each one? Encourage the pupils to explain how they sorted the materials. **What did you talk about when you were sorting the materials? Which ones were the hardest to sort? Why?** This may highlight specific examples of the pupils' understanding about materials. **Did any of you change your minds as you were sorting? What was it that made you change your thinking?** Encourage pupils to think about how they have been thinking about the issues. **How have you been thinking about these materials? How did that kind of thinking help you? What was making the task difficult? What have you learned about your thinking?** Encourage the pupils to reflect on and share any significant discussions that they had in their groups. Ask them to explain how these discussions changed their thinking.

Cognitive conflict and social construction: Part 2

- **We have thought about putting water into these items. What about turning the problem around? If these items were in water, how could we get the item and the water separated again? For example, if I have a bowl of sand and water, how can I get water in this bowl and sand in the other? If I put 2 teaspoons full of sugar in my tea, can I get them back again? Think about how to separate them and come up with an idea you agree on. When you have thought about this, think about a different item – one that needs to be separated from the water in a different way.** Give the groups long enough to work out at least 2 ways of separation.
- ***Class sharing:*** Ask each group to share one idea for separating sand and water. Encourage pupils to challenge and question each other. **I don't think that will work because ... Why do you think that ...?** Next, ask each group to share their ideas on the other item they chose. Again, encourage class discussion. Try to encourage the comments, questions and challenges to go around the class rather than through the teacher each time.

Metacognition (Whole class)

Encourage pupils to move from thinking about the *task* to thinking about their *thinking*. **How were you thinking about this problem? What helped you? What made it difficult? Did anyone say anything that was particularly helpful? Why was that helpful? What did you think as a result? If you had to do something like this again, what would you do differently?**

> ***Please note:*** **Keep the photocopies of Resource sheets 20 and 21 for use in Activity 4.3: Sorting out the Mix-ups.**

Schema

FACT BOX

Concrete modelling

ACTIVITIES 1.3 4.3 6.1

Introduction

Concrete modelling is the building of simple theoretical models that offer an explanation for observations. In concrete models, each element in the model has a specific concrete referent in reality.

Aim

Experience in concrete modelling will help the pupils to understand the relationships between a number of factors or variables, all of which are amenable to immediate perception because they are 'concrete' (that is, real).

Activity 1.3: What makes me Move? invites the pupils to think about links between bones, muscles and joints and how they work in conjunction with each other.

Activity 4.3: Sorting out the Mix-ups requires pupils to think about the properties of substances and how these influence the ways in which substances can be separated.

Activity 6.1: My Bulb won't Work requires pupils to think about how a circuit works and to devise a way of explaining it to someone who does not understand.

Solids and liquids **Activity 4.3**

Sorting out the Mix-ups

Aim

Pupils need to think about the properties and characteristics of the items so as to be able to separate them from each other and give reasons for the ways of separating.

Materials

Supplied

- Resource sheets 20 and 21: 2 photocopiable pages of cards, each page labelled with the names of 12 different substances (as used in **Activity 4.1: Where does it Belong?** and **Activity 4.2: I can't find the Sugar**).

Before you start

Look out the cards you used in **Activity 4.1: Where does it Belong?** and **Activity 4.2: I can't find the Sugar** or take photocopies of Resource sheets 20 and 21 – one for each group – and cut each photocopied sheet to make 12 substance cards.

Place a full set of 24 cards on each group's table

Activity

Concrete preparation

- Look again at the items on the cards. **What have we learned about these in the last few weeks?** Recap on the characteristics and properties that have been discussed.

Cognitive conflict and social construction: Part 1

- **We have looked at these items and grouped them in various ways. We have also thought about what happens when we add water. But what would happen if some of these things got mixed up together? For example, one day my friend left her little daughter in the kitchen. The little girl tipped all the sugar into the rice jar. How do you think my friend got the sugar back into its own jar again? Talk in your groups and come up with some ideas. When you have sorted that out, see if there are other items that you could separate in the same way if they had been mixed up.**
- Give the groups time to think about various ways of separating materials. Encourage class discussion of the ideas. **Why is it that the same method works for both these mix-ups? Why is this a good way to separate these 2 items? What makes this difficult? Do you think there is a better way to separate these items?**

Metacognition

It is important to encourage the pupils to think beyond the task and think about their thinking. **What did you have to think about as you did this task? What knowledge did you use to help you? What would have helped you to do this better?**

Cognitive conflict and social construction: Part 2

- Now the task is to look for 2 other items that need separating in a different way. **Are there other things that, if they were put together, you would have to separate using a different method?** Take a few ideas from around the class, then allow the groups time to develop their own ideas. When they have had enough time to discuss their ideas, tell them that this time when they share their plan they are not to mention the 2 items they start with. The rest of the class have to work out what is being separated as they listen to the clues given by the group. Now they need to think about the clues they will offer. The initial clues must not give too much away. As they work, listen to their ideas. Some groups may need some support.
- ***Class sharing:*** Start with the group that you think has most understood the task. Encourage the groups to wait to hear 3 clues before they offer a suggestion. You need to discourage guessing at all times. Any suggestion must be accompanied by a reason, e.g. *I think it is … and … because …* . We model this by the language we use. Always use 'think' not 'guess'.
- After the first group has finished, ask if any other group needs some more time. If so, give another few minutes. The group that went first can process what helped them to do this task.
- Give the other groups the opportunity to share their clues.

Metacognition

What were you thinking when you decided to [… develop your ideas in a certain way]**?** Bring to the pupils' attention any interesting ideas that you overheard during their group conversations. It is important that the pupils share these ideas and say why they are interesting. Encourage the pupils to move their thinking from thinking about the *task* to thinking about their *thinking*. **How were you thinking about this problem? What helped you? What made it difficult? Did anyone say anything that was particularly helpful? Why was that helpful? What did you think as a result? If you had to do something like this again, what would you do differently? Could you give a cook some useful advice about separating items that have got mixed up in the kitchen?**

Schema

FACT BOX

Causality

ACTIVITIES 2.2 2.3 5.1 5.2 6.3

Introduction

Causality is a special type of relationship between variables. What causes what? The confusion of correlation (things happening together) with *Causality* (one making the other happen) is a problem that besets even otherwise intelligent adults: the link between a cause and an effect is not always obvious. Three- and four-year-olds may suggest that 'The wind is caused by the trees waving back and forth'. Although few eight- and nine-year-olds are likely to hold this belief, the relationship between different variables may still be problematic.

Aim

The pupils are asked to explore *Causality* in a variety of contexts, such as the relationship between habitat and animal characteristics, or force and the subsequent movement.

Activity 2.2: How am I Adapted? encourages the pupils to develop an understanding of the relationship between animals' characteristics and the habitat in which they live.

Activity 2.3: What am I? explores the relationship between animals' characteristics and habitats in a game. Once the pupils have made the causal link, they are asked to use this to make predictions about unknown animals.

Activity 5.1: Where are the Forces? examines the causal relationships existing between the movement of an object/person and the forces being exerted.

Activity 5.2: Can you Change the Force? requires the pupils to explore this relationship further. They will think about which force to change and how to measure it. In the process they will discover some of the complexities of investigating forces with accuracy.

Activity 6.3: Controlling the Light requires pupils to think about the relationships between the bulb, the switch and the battery. They investigate the effects on the light when these are altered.

Friction **Activity 5.1**

Where are the Forces?

Aim

The aim is to challenge the pupils to consider and identify all the forces that are acting on a particular object.

Materials

Supplied

- Resource sheet 22, which is a photocopiable page of cards describing situations where forces are being exerted. The first 4 cards are labelled A1–A4; the remaining 8 are B1–B8.

Before you start

Take photocopies of Resource sheet 22 – one for each group – then cut each sheet to make 12 situations cards.

Activity

Concrete preparation

- Give each group the cards labelled A1, A2, A3 and A4. Ensure that pupils can read the words. Ask the pupils in their groups to ensure that each pupil understands what is happening in each situation. Check whether there are any words that pupils are still not sure about. Add to their explanations, if necessary. Pupils discuss in their groups. They can draw a sketch of the situation. Explain that this just needs to be a quick line-drawing to give the idea: there is not time for detailed drawings.

Cognitive conflict and social construction: Part 1

- Ask the pupils to identify all the forces acting on the things in the cards. They will need to agree reasons for their choices. They may find a way to represent the forces on the cards.
- ***Class sharing:*** Ask each group what forces they identified on each card, e.g. (card A2):

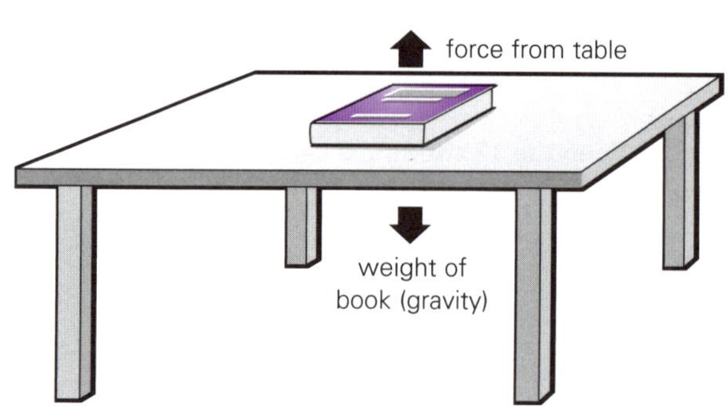

What forces did you identify in the situation on card A1? Did any group think something different? Identify on the whiteboard or OHT all the forces mentioned. Encourage the pupils to discuss similarities and differences between the items. Repeat this for each card. If there are discrepancies and disagreements the groups may need more time to talk before discussing again in the whole class group. The groups may need to discuss some issues to become clear about their confusions and then bring them to the class group.

- **Which forces are we sure about? Why? What forces do we need to know more about? Why? What is it we are not sure about? Pupils work together, again in their groups, to identify the forces if necessary.** Pupils may use words like *gravity, friction, air resistance*, but encourage them to explain what they think the words mean. Pupils may use words without having any real sense of their meaning.

Metacognition

Encourage the pupils to explain some of the ideas they discussed – some that caused disagreement, some that they could not resolve. Ask if anybody changed their mind about anything. What enabled them to do this? Encourage pupils to question each other to develop understanding. **What did you have to think about when you were identifying the forces? What was difficult about this task? What helped you to do this? Have you done anything before that helped you in this task? Is there anything you have learnt from this that you think you could use in another task? Did anybody show you anything that helped you to understand a force differently?**

Cognitive conflict and social construction: Part 2

- Give out cards B1–B8, which pupils may find more difficult. They again try to identify all the forces operating on the items. Remind pupils to think about some of the ideas that came up in the class sharing session. Give groups enough time to agree on their ideas. Ask them to choose a different person to feed back the ideas. It is important that everybody understands.
- ***Class discussion:*** Encourage each group to share their ideas. Start with a different group for each new card being discussed. Give time for pupils to question, challenge, agree and disagree with each other. Try to create class discussion rather than ideas being mediated through you, the teacher. **In which situations are similar things happening? Where are there different forces at work?** It is not necessary to discuss every scenario. Choose some that pupils have spent time over in discussion. It is more important to use the most relevant, conflicting and interesting rather than feeling that you have to use them all.

Metacognition (Whole class)

It is important to give pupils the opportunity to discuss what is difficult or what forces they do not understand. This can then become the focus of subsequent science lessons so that their understanding can develop through investigations. **What made this difficult? Was any card particularly difficult? Why was this? What did you think about to solve the difficulty? What had you learnt before that helped you? Is there anything you do at home or in the park that helps you to understand what is going on here? What would have helped you to do this task more easily?**

Please note: **Keep the 12 situations cards made using Resource sheet 22 for use in Activity 5.2: Can you Change the Force?**

Schema

FACT BOX

Causality

ACTIVITIES 2.2 2.3 5.1 5.2 6.3

Introduction

Causality is a special type of relationship between variables. What causes what? The confusion of correlation (things happening together) with *Causality* (one making the other happen) is a problem that besets even otherwise intelligent adults: the link between a cause and an effect is not always obvious. Three- and four-year-olds may suggest that 'The wind is caused by the trees waving back and forth'. Although few eight- and nine-year-olds are likely to hold this belief, the relationship between different variables may still be problematic.

Aim

The pupils are asked to explore *Causality* in a variety of contexts, such as the relationship between habitat and animal characteristics, or force and the subsequent movement.

Activity 2.2: How am I Adapted? encourages the pupils to develop an understanding of the relationship between animals' characteristics and the habitats in which they live.

Activity 2.3: What am I? explores the relationship between characteristics and habitat in a game. Once the pupils have made the causal link, they are asked to use this to make predictions about unknown animals.

Activity 5.1: Where are the Forces? examines the causal relationships existing between the movement of an object/person and the forces being exerted.

Activity 5.2: Can you Change the Force? requires the pupils to explore this relationship further. They will think about which force to change and how to measure it. In the process they will discover some of the complexities of investigating forces with accuracy.

Activity 6.3: Controlling the Light requires pupils to think about the relationships between the bulb, the switch and the battery. They investigate the effects on the light when these are altered.

Friction **Activity 5.2**

Can you Change the Force?

Aim

The pupils will consider the relationship between the movement and the amount of force that is exerted on an object.

Materials

Supplied

- Resource sheet 22, which is a photocopiable page of cards describing situations where forces are being exerted. The first 4 cards are labelled A1–A4 and the remaining 8 are labelled B1–B8.

Before you start

Look out the cards you used in **Activity 5.1: Where are the Forces?** or take photocopies of Resource sheet 22 – one for each group – then cut each sheet to make 12 situations cards.

Activity

Concrete preparation

- Give each group a set of cards, as used in the last activity (situations cards A1–A4 and B1–B8). Ask the pupils to talk in their groups about what they learnt last time. Did they learn anything new? Give them the opportunity to make a few comments.

Cognitive conflict and social construction: Part 1

- **In most of the situations described on the cards there is a moving object/person. How would you describe the movement?** (e.g. *falling, dropping, pushing, pulling, climbing*). Give each group the opportunity to discuss movement words. Ask them to share what they think. Ask them to give reasons for their choice.
- ***Class sharing:*** Encourage a discussion of reasons. Discuss any differences and similarities in the pupils' choices.
- **How could we alter any of the forces in each case?** Give the groups time to discuss their different ideas about which forces they could alter and how they think they could do this. Encourage the pupils to share their ideas with the class.
- ***Class sharing:*** Give each group the opportunity to explain how they think they could alter the forces in one card. Pupils sit in

their groups, but in a position where they can see as many other pupils as possible. When each group has shared, encourage class discussion of the ideas. Encourage the groups to challenge each other by questioning. **We don't think that because … Why do you think … ?** If pupils use words like *friction*, *resistance*, *measure*, write them on the whiteboard and challenge pupils to explain them. **Resistance … Do we all know what that means?** In this way you have the opportunity to formatively assess their understanding and this will inform the teaching that is needed in subsequent activities. **Why do you think we would want to change the force? What advantage is there in being able to alter a force?**

Metacognition

The pupils should by now be familiar with getting in touch with their thinking. They should be able to explain why this activity is helpful for them in developing their thinking further. Try to ensure that all the pupils are engaging in this activity. **Can you think who might need to consider some of these issues? What kind of job do you think these issues are important for? What made it difficult to think about these things? What helped you? What would have helped you more? When do you think you could use some of the ideas that we have discussed today?** Finish by asking each group to agree a question for further investigation. Each group could choose or be given a different card to focus on.

Schema

FACT BOX

Relationship between variables

ACTIVITIES 3.2 5.3

Introduction

'The stronger the wind, the faster I can walk to school.' Is that true? In other words, is there a relationship between the variable 'strength of wind' and the variable 'how fast one can walk'? Science is all about exploring relationships between variables and two activities in this programme give pupils an opportunity to do just that.

Aim

The pupils are encouraged to identify and consider the relationships between different events or processes. It is not just a case of *whether* things 'go together' but *how* they go together: as one goes up, does the other go up too, or go down, or isn't it connected at all?

Activity 3.2: Hotter or Colder? requires the pupils to consider changes in temperature over a period of time.

Activity 5.3: Late for School invites pupils to consider the effect of the wind on the speed at which they can walk.

Friction **Activity 5.3**

Late for School

Aim

The pupils will consider the relationship between the strength and direction of the wind and the speed at which we might walk.

Materials

None required.

Activity

Concrete preparation

- **Think about walking to school, or running in a park or by the sea. What can you feel? What can you hear?** Take a few ideas. Try to get as wide a range of ideas as possible.

Cognitive conflict and social construction: Part 1

- **One day when I was in school early getting things ready for you, I noticed some children in the playground. I went out and asked them why they were so early. They said they were early because it was very windy. Later on we were in class, the register was finished, the dinner book was finished and we had started some work when some children came in. I asked, 'Why are you late for school?' They said, 'We're late because of the wind.' I was confused. How could it be that some children were early because of the wind and some were late because of the wind? I thought maybe you might have some ideas about this to help me.** Listen to some of their ideas.
- **How could we find out what really went on that day? Can you devise an investigation that would help us to be sure what was going on?** Give the groups time to work out what they would need to do to find out. Some groups may need support in working this out. How will they record what they do? What will they have discovered when their investigation is complete? Give each group the opportunity to share their plan. Invite other groups to comment, ask questions or add ideas. Give the groups time to revise their plans in the light of the discussion.
- Give the groups time to talk about what may have been going on. They may want to make some sketches or diagrams to aid their explanations.
- ***Class sharing:*** Pupils need to sit where they can see as many others as possible. Encourage each group to express their ideas and explanations. Nobody should challenge until all the original ideas are heard. Ask the groups: **Are you adding to an existing idea or coming up with a new idea?** They should avoid repeating something already said. When the ideas have been shared, they can begin to question and challenge.

Metacognition

Ask pupils how they are thinking about this problem. **Is there a better way to think about it? How would that method be better? Have we done anything before that we could use to help us with this problem?**

Cognitive conflict and social construction: Part 2

- Give each group the opportunity to conduct their investigation, record it and discuss their results. If the weather is not windy, they may come up with ways of creating a wind (e.g. blowing, a fan, a hairdryer).
- ***Class sharing:*** Each group tells the class the main point they have learnt by conducting their investigation, using their results as the evidence. Discourage *description* of the investigation as you want to focus on *analysis of results* for learning. Encourage other groups to question and challenge ideas.

Metacognition

Make the main elements of learning as conscious as possible. Identify these main elements and encourage pupils to clarify what they had to think about, consider and apply in order to learn. **What did you have to think about in the planning of your investigation? What did that result lead you to consider? What did that teach you? What have you learned about devising an investigation? What things did you have to consider? How did the other groups help you? What made this really difficult? If you are out on the playground conducting your investigation, how would you explain to the headteacher what you were doing? What questions do you have now about conducting an investigation? What good advice could you give the class next year so they do a good job on this lesson?**

Schema

FACT BOX

Concrete modelling

ACTIVITIES 1.3 4.3 6.1

Introduction

Concrete modelling is the building of simple theoretical models that offer an explanation for observations. In concrete models, each element in the model has a specific concrete referent in reality.

Aim

Experience in concrete modelling will help the pupils to understand the relationships between a number of factors or variables, all of which are amenable to immediate perception because they are 'concrete' (that is, real).

Activity 1.3: What makes me Move? invites the pupils to think about links between bones, muscles and joints and how they work in conjunction with each other.

Activity 4.3: Sorting out the Mix-ups requires pupils to think about the properties of substances and how these influence the ways in which substances can be separated.

Activity 6.1: My Bulb won't Work requires pupils to think about how a circuit works and to devise a way of explaining it to someone who does not understand.

Circuits and conductors

Activity 6.1

My Bulb won't Work

Aim

The pupils will be challenged to think about what is needed to make a bulb light and then to construct a model of a circuit using their bodies. They will sketch their ideas. They will then try to make a 'living' circuit, while thinking about how to switch the light on and off and to vary the brightness of the bulb.

Materials

Not supplied

- One small electric light bulb, e.g. torch bulb.
- One large sheet of paper and a marker pen for each group.

Health and safety

Remind the pupils that electricity can be dangerous and should be handled with care. This applies to all three activities within the topic.

Activity

Concrete preparation (Whole class)

- Pupils think about what is necessary to make a bulb work. Hold up the light bulb for all to see. Ask: **What do I need to get this bulb to light?** Pupils discuss in their groups. Give them the opportunity to share their ideas.

Cognitive conflict and social construction: Part 1

- **Work out together what you need and how to make this bulb work.** The pupils can draw a sketch to illustrate their ideas. Explain that this just needs to be a quick line-drawing to give the idea, as there is not time for detailed drawings.
- The groups may want to clarify some issues before bringing them to the class group. They may need to sit on the carpet so they can see the sketches. Ask each group to show their sketch and describe their ideas. When each group has explained and displayed their sketch, ask if anybody has any questions, comments or challenges.
- The main element to be clear about is that both a *source of power* and a *complete circuit* are required. **What is a circuit? Do you understand that description? Can you explain it in another way? Do you agree with that idea? Can you explain what you disagree with?**

Metacognition

Encourage the pupils to explain some of the ideas they discussed, some that caused disagreement, some that they could not resolve. Ask if anybody changed their mind about anything. What enabled them to do this? Encourage the pupils to question each other to develop their understanding. **What did you have to think about when you were drawing the circuits? What was difficult about this task? What helped you to do this? Have you done anything before that helped you in this task? Is there anything you have learnt from this that you think you could use in another task? Did anybody show you anything that helped you to understand a circuit differently?**

Cognitive conflict and social construction: Part 2

- Ask each group to use themselves as pieces of equipment to make a working circuit (i.e. one pupil will pretend to be the bulb, one the battery, etc.) Ask them to think about making the bulb light up, go off, be bright, not be bright.
- ***Class sharing:*** Give the groups time to discuss their different ideas. Encourage the pupils to share their ideas in the class group. Pupils sit in their groups but in a position where they can see the other groups' ideas. Each group gets the opportunity to show the ideas they have come up with. Encourage discussion of reasons. Give each group the opportunity to explain what they think.
- When each group has shared, encourage class discussion of the ideas. Encourage the groups to challenge each other by questioning. **We don't think that because ... Why do you think ... ?** In this way, you will have the opportunity to formatively assess their understanding and this will inform the teaching needed in subsequent activities. Discuss any differences and similarities in the pupils' ideas.

Metacognition

Try to encourage the focus of this discussion to stay on the thinking. Pupils tend to want to discuss social/behaviour issues, e.g. *X did not want to be the bulb/hold hands*. Model for them that you are more interested in the thinking and learning and that these are your priorities. **What made this difficult? Was anything particularly difficult? Why was this? What did you think about to solve the difficulty? What had you learnt before that helped you? Is there anything you do at home or in the park that helps you to understand what is going on here? What would have helped you to do this task more easily?**

Schema

FACT BOX

Classification

ACTIVITIES 1.1 1.2 2.1 3.1 4.1 6.2

Introduction

To understand pupils' difficulties with the process of *Classification*, you need to understand two ideas: variables and values. A *variable* is simply a way in which things vary from one another. Colour, shape and number of legs are all variables. Each variable may have a number of values. The variable 'colour' may have the *values* blue, green, red, etc. *Classification* problems become more difficult for pupils as the number of variables increases, and as the number of values of each variable increases.

Aim

Even elementary work on living and non-living things requires them to be put into groups with some characteristics in common: that is, to be classified. *Classification* problems can be graded in difficulty according to how many variables are involved, how many values each variable has, and how clearly defined each set is within the classification.

Activity 1.1: Who am I? invites the pupils to make links between the shapes of animals and their skeletons.

Activity 1.2: All these Bones requires the pupils to classify different human bones according to various criteria, e.g. shape, function, strength.

Activity 2.1: Where do I Live? requires the pupils to classify animals according to their native habitats.

Activity 3.1: How Hot are You? invites the pupils to classify scenarios according to given temperatures and match these to the thermometers given.

Activity 4.1: Where does it Belong? asks the pupils to consider criteria for grouping various substances with an emphasis on solids and liquids.

Activity 6.2: Do I Work? is an activity where pupils identify those circuits that make a bulb light up.

Circuits and conductors

Activity 6.2

Do I Work?

Aim

The aim is to challenge the pupils to look at diagrams of circuits and discuss which they think would make the bulbs light. They discuss ways of making other circuits work. They then discuss what happens when various materials are inserted into the circuits.

Materials

Supplied

- Resource sheet 23, which shows diagrams for 12 different electrical circuits.

Not supplied

- One each of: a cork, paper, a paperclip, a penny, a soup spoon, some cotton wool, a tissue, some kitchen foil.

Before you start

Take photocopies of Resource sheet 23 – one for each group – then cut each sheet to make 12 circuit cards. The circuits where the bulbs are lit are: 1, 2, 3, 6, 7, 8, 9 and 10.

Activity

Concrete preparation

Remind pupils of the standard symbols used in diagrams of circuits (see below). Ask: **Why do we need standard symbols?**

Name	Symbol
wire	
battery	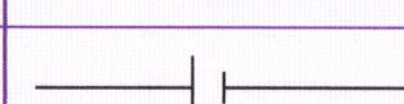
open switch	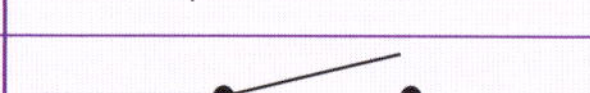
closed switch	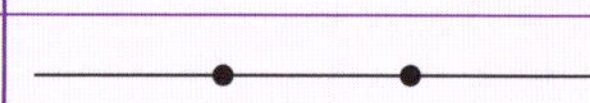
bulb	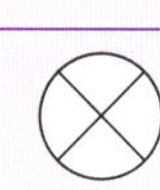

Cognitive conflict and social construction: Part 1 (Groups)

- Give each group a copy of the circuit cards made from Resource sheet 23. Discuss and identify which of these will light the bulb as they are. Encourage the pupils to discuss similarities and differences between the circuits as they work together in their groups to identify the circuits that they think will work. Remind them to think about their reasons.
- Ask each group what they thought for each circuit.
- ***Class sharing:*** Ask each group to choose one circuit to explain so that each one is explained for the class. If there are discrepancies and disagreements the groups may need more time to talk before discussing again in the whole class group. **Which circuits are we sure about? Why? What circuits do we need to think more about? Why? What is it we are not sure about? What do we need to do to get the other circuits to light the bulb?**

Metacognition

Encourage the pupils to discuss how they are thinking about this activity. **What is helping us? Have we some ideas that are causing us a problem? What can we do? How do we change our ideas?**

Cognitive conflict and social construction: Part 2

- **Here I have a collection of objects** (i.e. a cork, paper, a paperclip, a penny, a soup spoon, some cotton wool, a tissue, some kitchen foil). **What do you think will happen to the bulb if I put each one of these, one at a time, into the circuit?** Give each group the opportunity to discuss their hypothesis. Ask them to record their ideas in some way.
- Ask the groups to share what they think. Ask them to give reasons for their ideas. If pupils use words like *conductor* or *insulator*, write them on the whiteboard and challenge pupils to explain them. ***Conductor*** **... Do we all know what that means? How can we find out if our ideas about altering the forces are accurate?**

Metacognition

What have we been thinking about today? Have you changed your mind about anything? Who helped you? How did that happen? Finish by asking each group to think about what they would like to investigate further.

Schema

FACT BOX

Causality

ACTIVITIES 2.2 2.3 5.1 5.2 6.3

Introduction

Causality is a special type of relationship between variables. What causes what? The confusion of correlation (things happening together) with *Causality* (one making the other happen) is a problem that besets even otherwise intelligent adults: the link between a cause and an effect is not always obvious. Three- and four-year-olds may suggest that 'The wind is caused by the trees waving back and forth'. Although few eight- and nine-year-olds are likely to hold this belief, the relationship between different variables may still be problematic.

Aim

The pupils are asked to explore *Causality* in a variety of contexts, such as the relationship between habitat and animal characteristics, or force and subsequent movement.

Activity 2.2: How am I Adapted? encourages the pupils to develop an understanding of the relationship between animals' characteristics and the habitat in which they live.

Activity 2.3: What am I? explores the relationship between characteristics and habitat in a game. Once the pupils have made the causal link, they are asked to use this to make predictions about unknown animals.

Activity 5.1: Where are the Forces? examines the causal relationships existing between the movement of an object/person and the forces being exerted.

Activity 5.2: Can you Change the Force? requires the pupils to explore this relationship further. They will think about which force to change and how to measure it. In the process they will discover some of the complexities of investigating forces with accuracy.

Activity 6.3: Controlling the Light requires pupils to think about the relationships between the bulb, the switch and the battery. They investigate the effects on the light when these are altered.

Circuits and conductors

Activity 6.3

Controlling the Light

Aim

The pupils will think about how to make a bulb go on/off and brighter/dimmer. This connects with work completed in **Activity 6.1: My Bulb won't Work** and **Activity 6.2: Do I Work?** as well linking with other science activities.

Materials

Supplied

- Resource sheet 24, which is a line-drawing of a monster's face – or you may prefer to do your own drawing.

Not supplied

- For each group: the components of an electrical circuit: battery/ies, bulb/s, a switch and some wire; rough paper and pencils; an empty cereal box and some glue, if required.

Before you start

Take photocopies of Resource sheet 25 – one for each group – enlarged to A3 if you wish, or draw your own monster. You could cut a hole in each sheet, where the monster's nose is, so that the pupils can push the bulb through it from underneath.

Activity

Concrete preparation

- **Talk in your groups for a few minutes and decide on the 3 most important things you have learnt during the last few weeks about making a bulb work.** Give each group the opportunity to share its key ideas. Take one idea from each group in turn. Remind pupils that they should not repeat an idea that has already been voiced. Ensure that the following key ideas have been covered: a circuit needs to be *complete* for a bulb to work; a circuit needs a *source of power*, the light can be *switched on/off* by *completing/breaking the circuit*; the *brightness* of the light can be *controlled*.

Cognitive conflict and social construction: Part 1 (Groups)

- **I have here a drawing of a monster's face. I want you to talk in your groups about how to give him a nose that can light up when someone plays with it. Work out together what**

you need to do, what materials you need and how you are going to do it. Draw a quick sketch of your design. Label all that you need. Give the groups rough paper and pencils and allow them sufficient time to complete the sketch.

- ***Class sharing:*** Ask each group to share their plans. After each one, ask if there are any questions or ideas that would help the group to improve its plan. Encourage the pupils to think of questions that will help in the detail of the planning.
- When each group has had the opportunity to share, allow the pupils to make their circuit and fix it to (or beneath) the monster's face, with the bulb positioned as his nose. The face could be glued to an empty cereal box, to make it more sturdy. When they have finished, each group demonstrates how their monster's nose lights up and switches off.

Metacognition

As the pupils demonstrate, they are explaining what they did and how their monster's nose works. Ask questions, and encourage the pupils to ask questions as well. **What did you have to think about to make this work? What was difficult? Did the order in which you did things matter? Why was this? Did you try something that did not work? How did you solve the problem? Did anybody change their mind about anything as you did this? What helped that to happen?**

Cognitive conflict and social construction: Part 2

- **Now think about this monster. If you want to make it a more exciting toy, what could you do? Talk in your groups about how you think you might do this.** Groups might think about making the nose flash, brighten or dim, add lighting eyes etc. **Work out together what you need to do, what equipment you need and how you are going to do it. Draw a quick sketch of your design. Label all that you need.** Give the groups time to complete this. Ask each group to share their plans. After each one, ask if there are any questions that would help that group to make their plan better. Encourage the pupils to think of questions that will help in the detail of the planning.
- ***Class sharing:*** When each group has had the opportunity to share, allow them time to adjust their plans in the light of what they now think. Give them the opportunity to try out their ideas. When they have finished, each group demonstrates what their monster can do.

Metacognition

Encourage the pupils to explain the ideas they discussed, some that caused difficulty or tension between them, some that they resolved and some that were not resolved. Encourage them to reflect on their learning together. **What did you have to change? I notice that you have used 2 circuits for eyes, could you have done something else? How did you get 2 eyes working on one circuit? Can you explain why your monster has 2 different-looking eyes? How could you change that? What did you have to think about to get the nose to dim? What did you know already that helped you to complete this task? What have you learnt today that is new? How did you learn that? Where do you think you would use these ideas? What did you need to know about bulbs/batteries that helped you? Why did that help you? What have we been thinking about today? Have you changed your mind about anything? Who helped you? How did that happen?**

Let's Think through Science! 8 & 9

Resource Section

The pages that follow contain these Resource sheets:

continued

15 How Hot are You? 1 (Activity 3.1)
This A3 Resource sheet may be found at the back of the book.

16 How Hot are You? 2 (Activity 3.1)

17 How Hot are You? 3 (Activity 3.1)

18 How Hot are You? 4 (Activity 3.1)

19 Hotter or Colder? (Activity 3.2)

20 Solids and Liquids 1 (Activities 4.1, 4.2, 4.3)

21 Solids and Liquids 2 (Activities 4.1, 4.2, 4.3)

22 Friction (Activities 5.1, 5.2)

23 Do I Work? (Activity 6.2)

24 Controlling the Light (Activity 6.3)

Resource sheet 1: Climb that Mountain

Mount Sharp
Total:

Mount Steep
Total:

Mount Rough
Total:

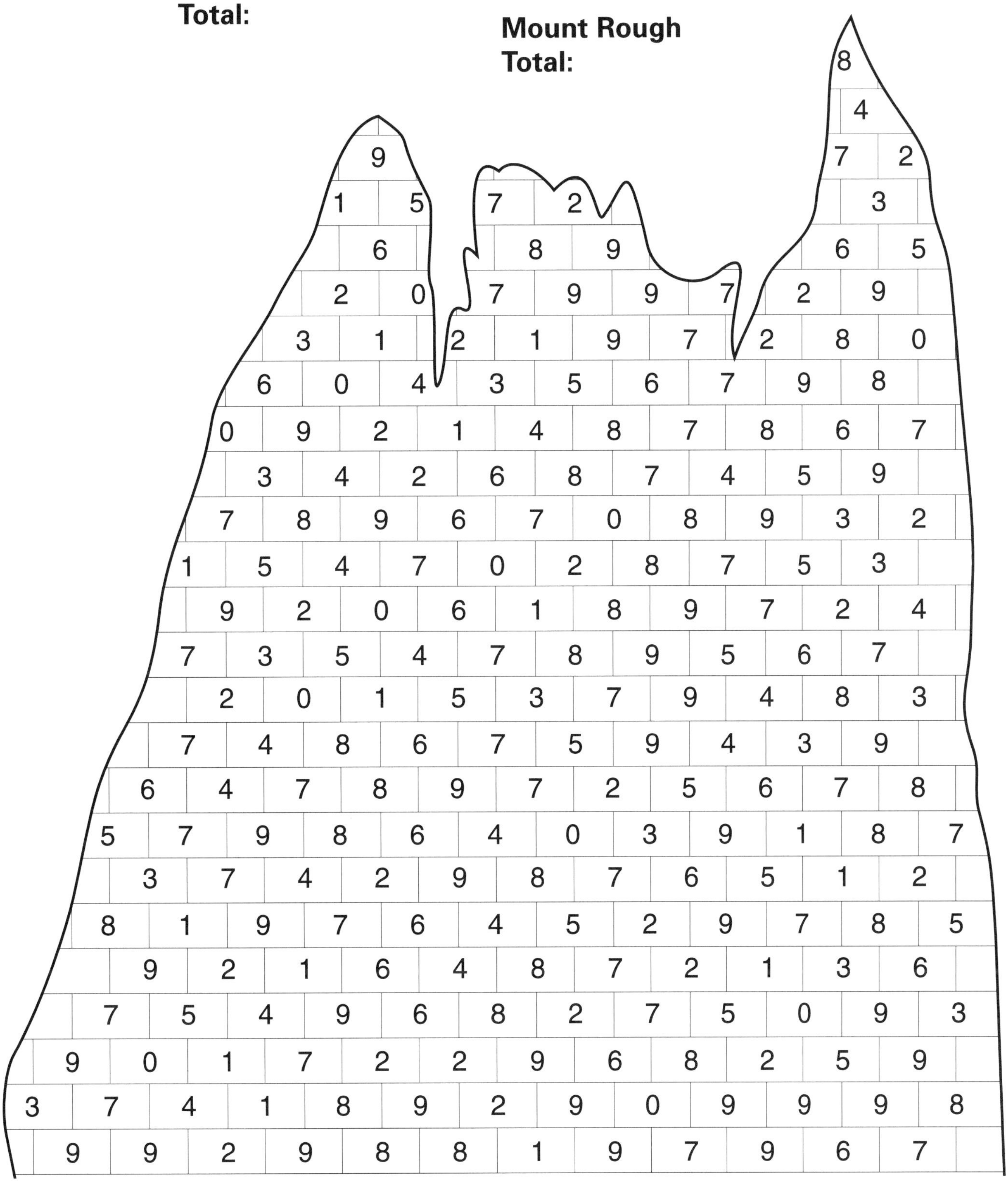

Start

Resource sheet 2: Make that Box

esource sheet 3: Who am I? 1

1

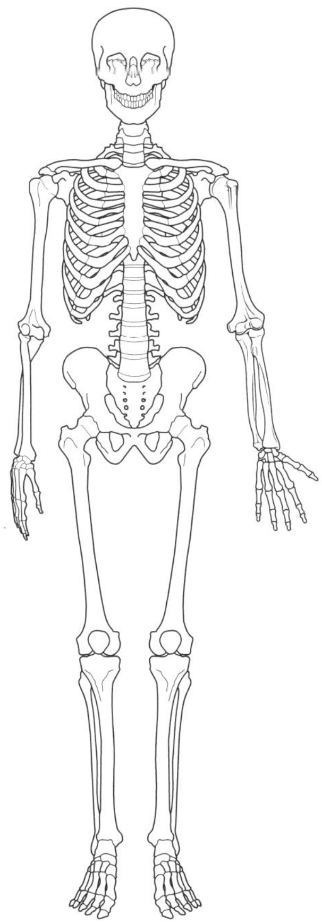

2

3

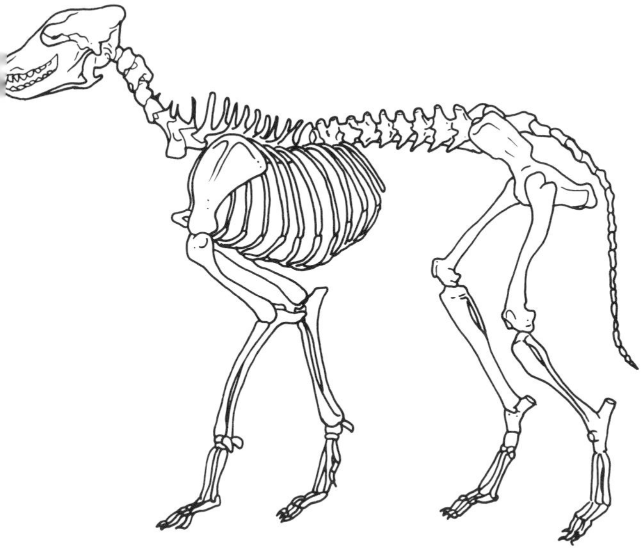

4

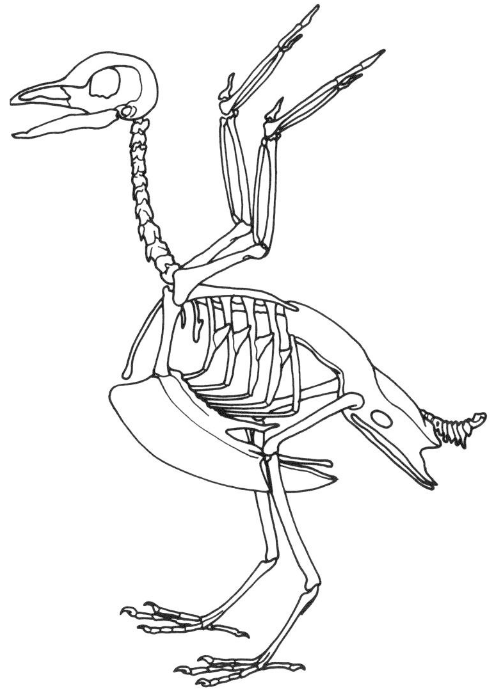

Resource sheet 4: Who am I? 2

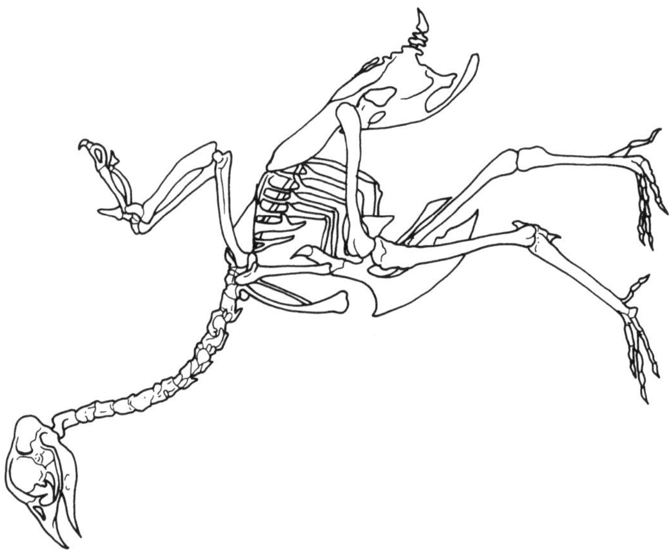

9

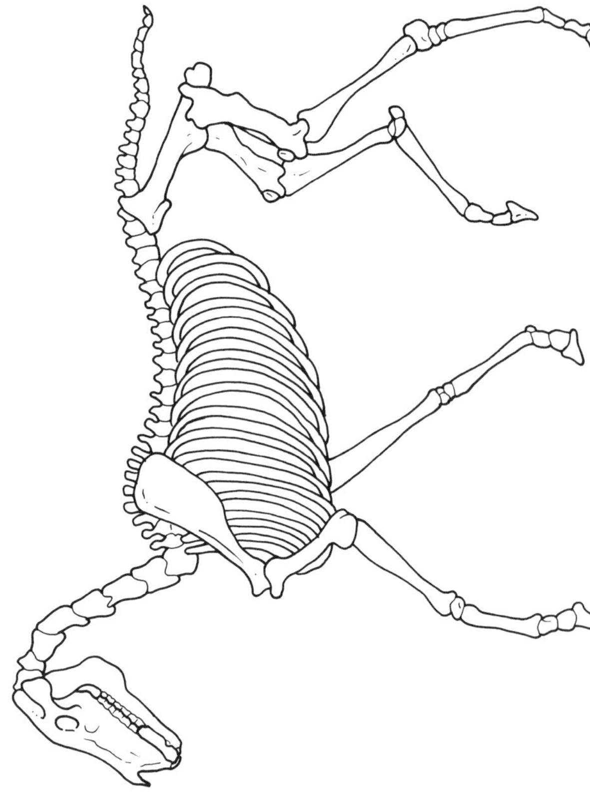

8

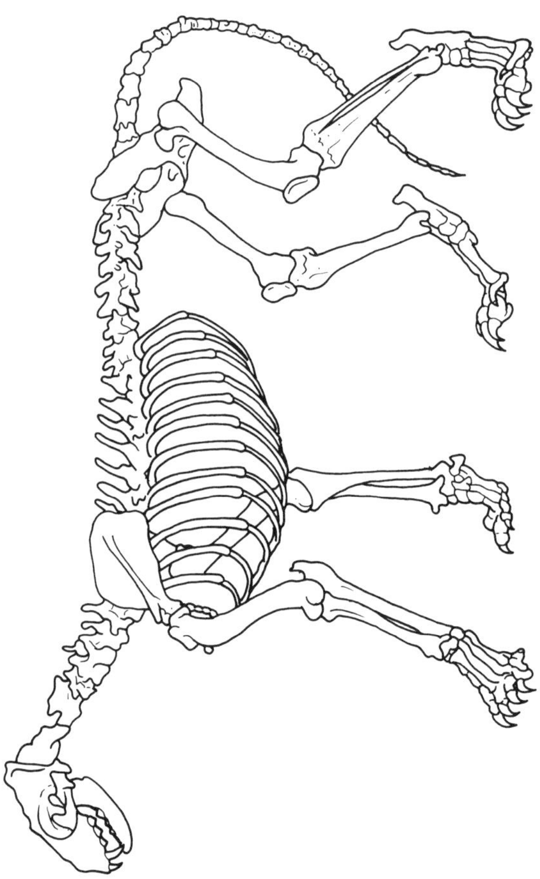

5

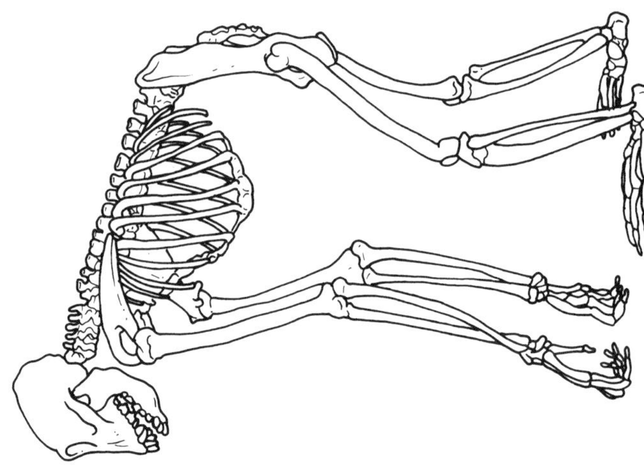

7

Resource sheet 5: Who am I? 3

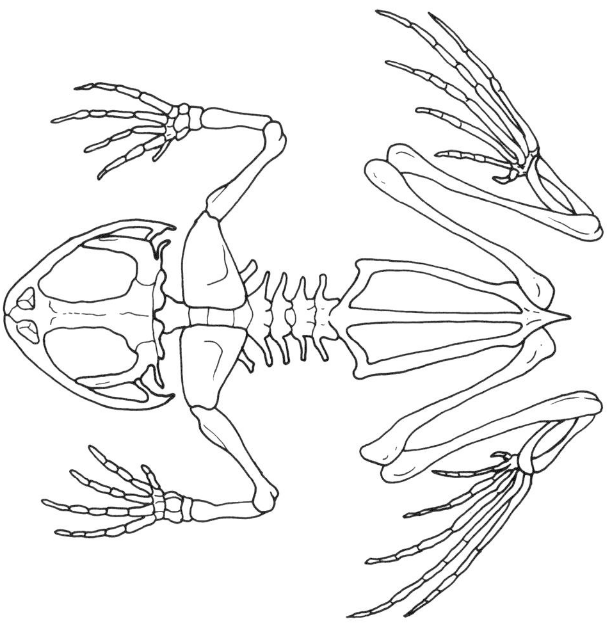

10

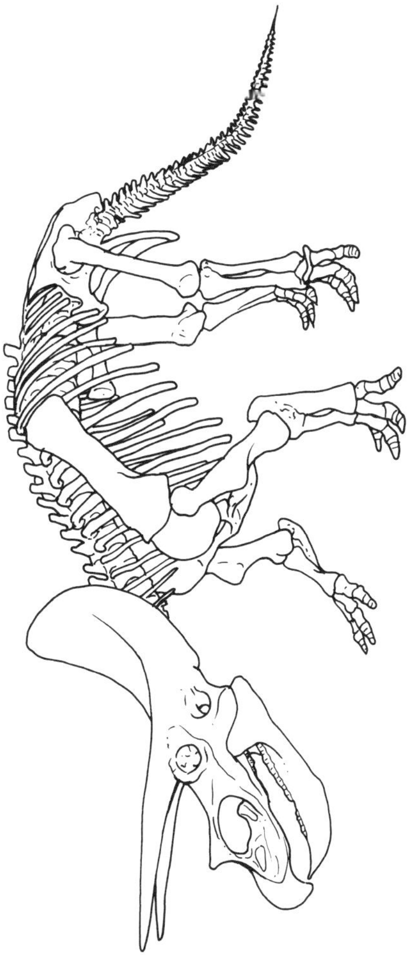

12

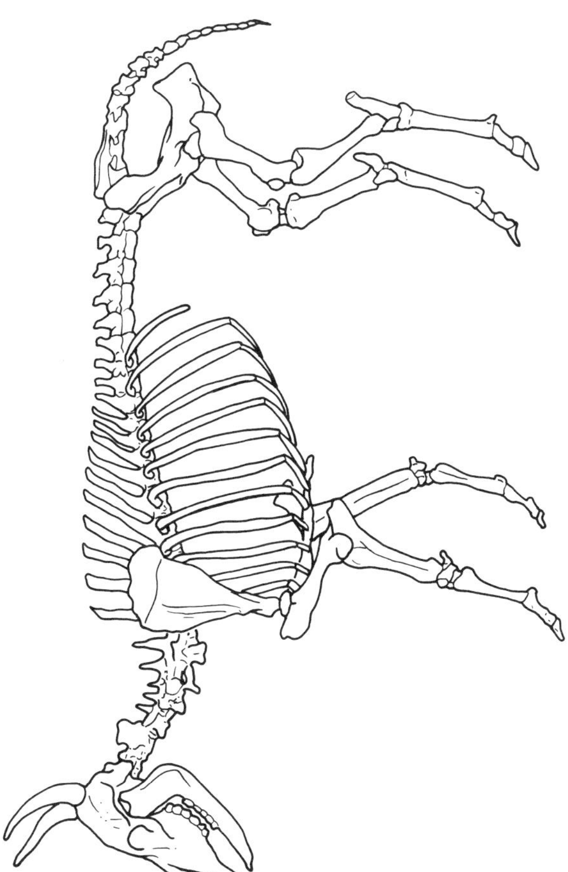

9

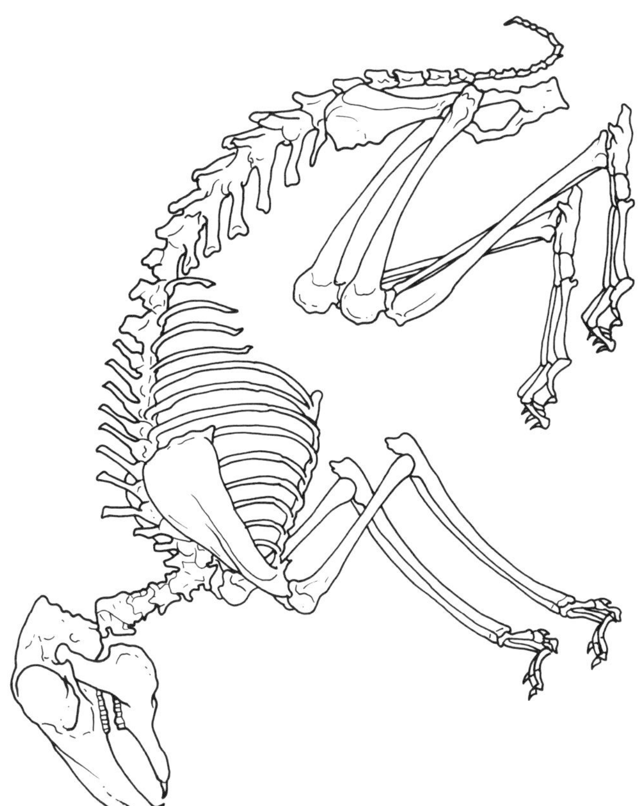

11

Resource sheet 6: Who am I? 4

13

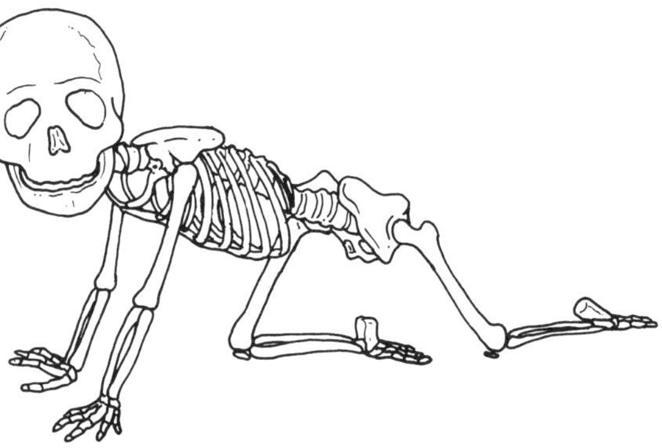

14

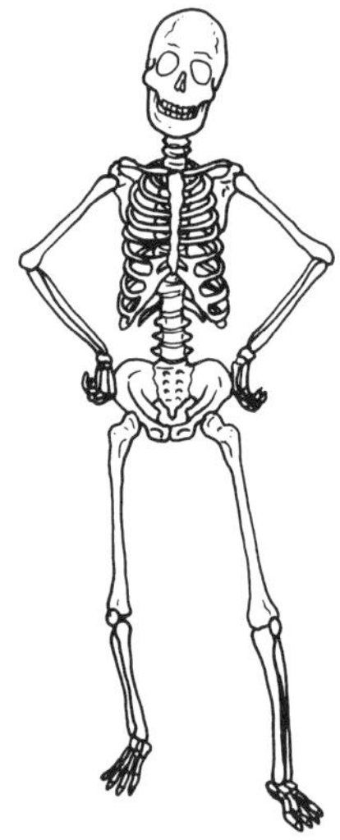

15

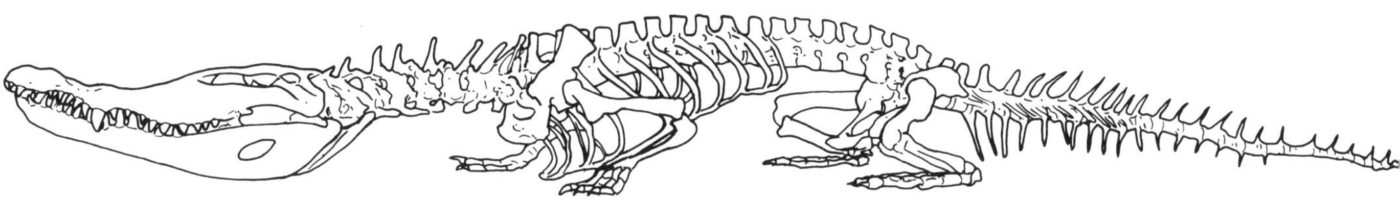

16

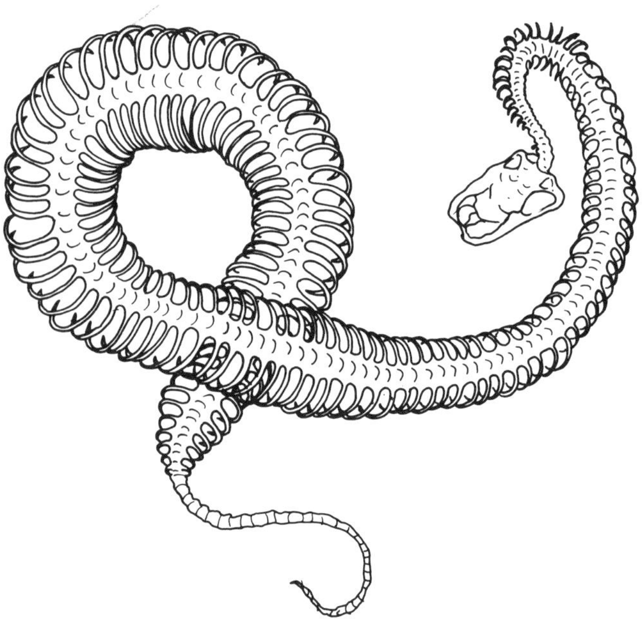

17

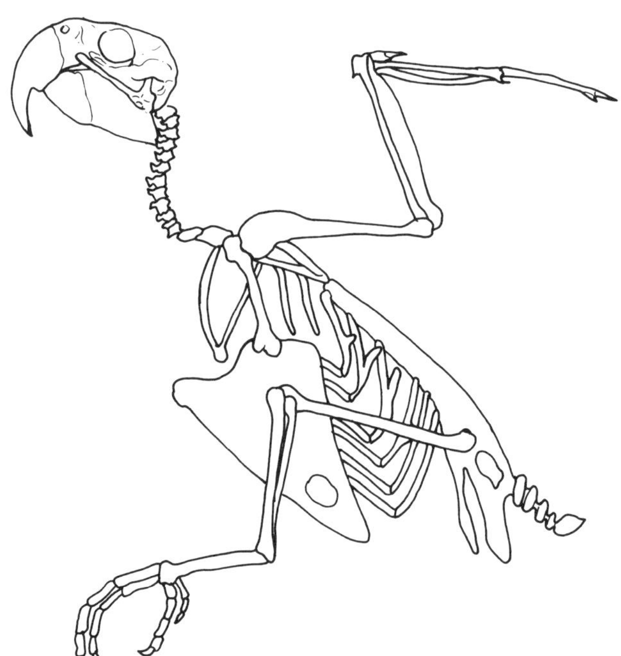

Resource sheet 7: All these Bones 1

2

3

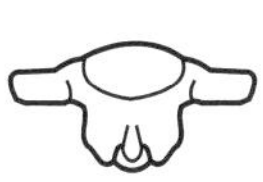

5

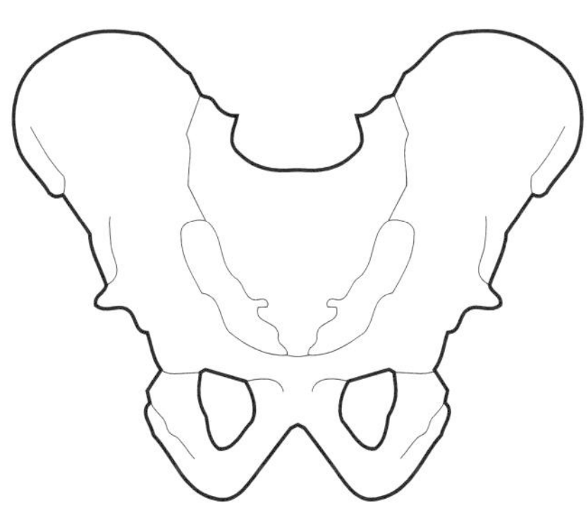

6

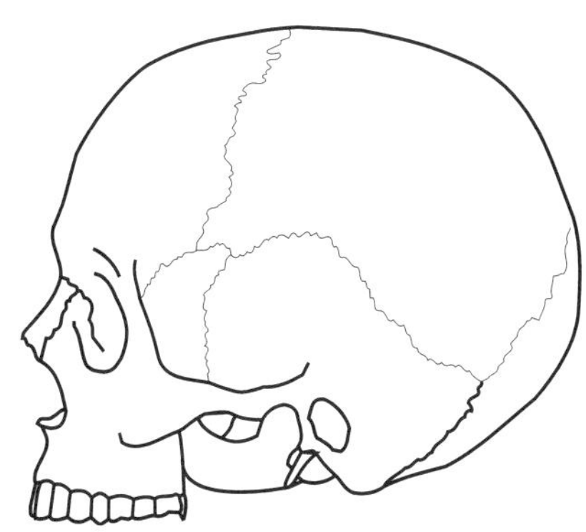

Resource sheet 8: All these Bones 2

7

8

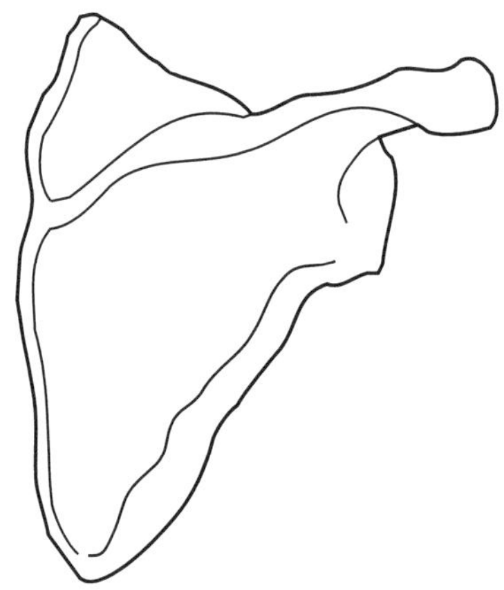

9

10

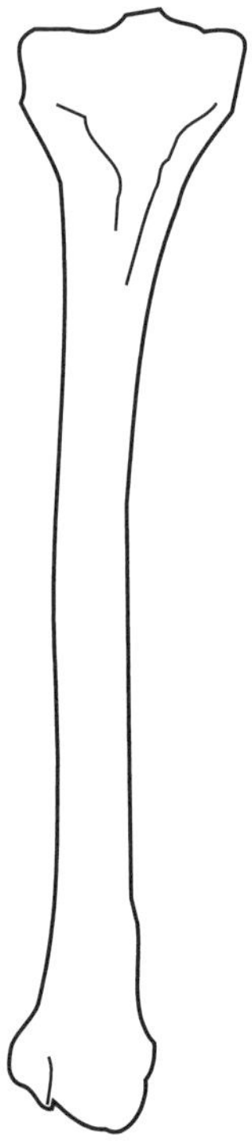

11

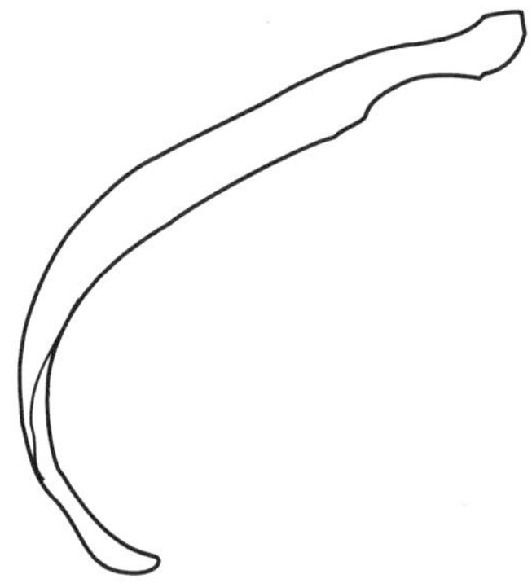

12

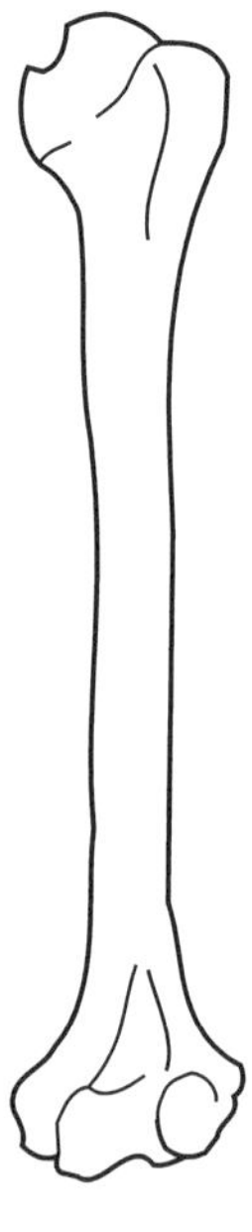

esource sheet 9: Where do I live? 1

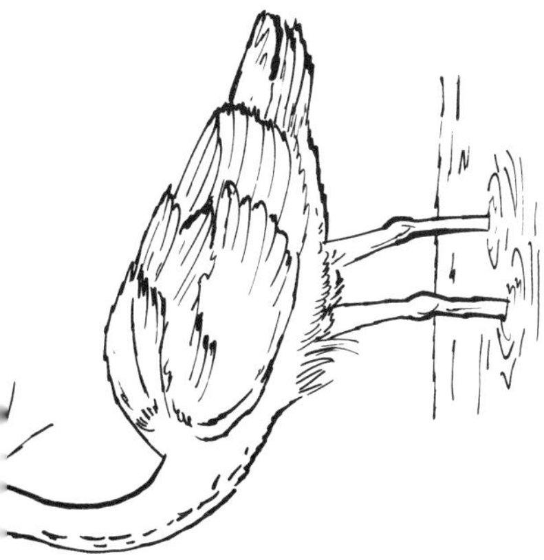

2

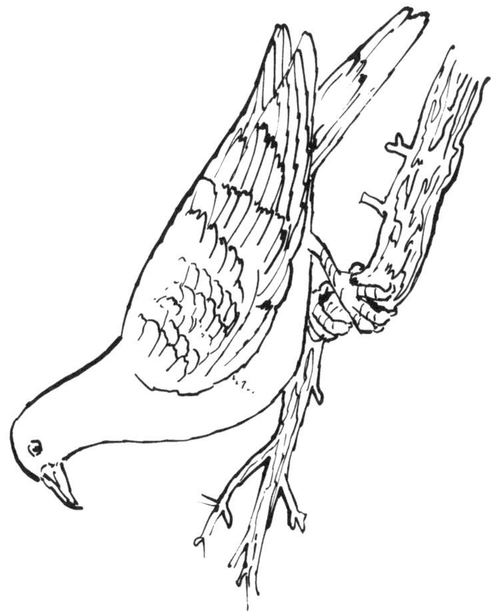

4

6

1

3

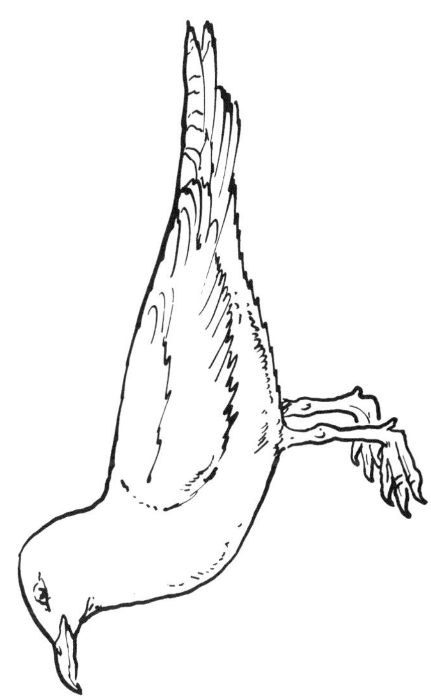

5

Resource sheet 10: Where do I Live? 2

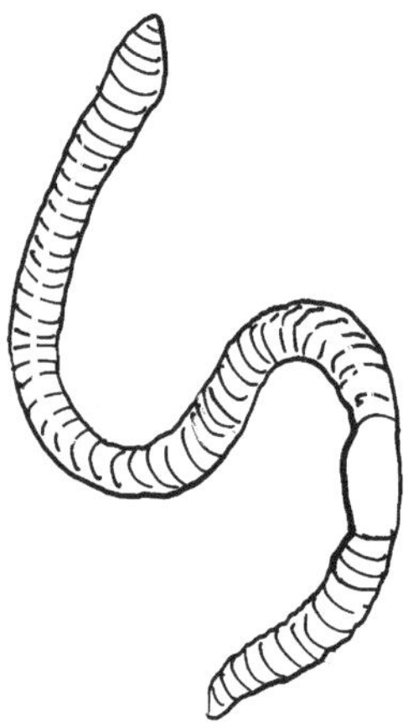

8

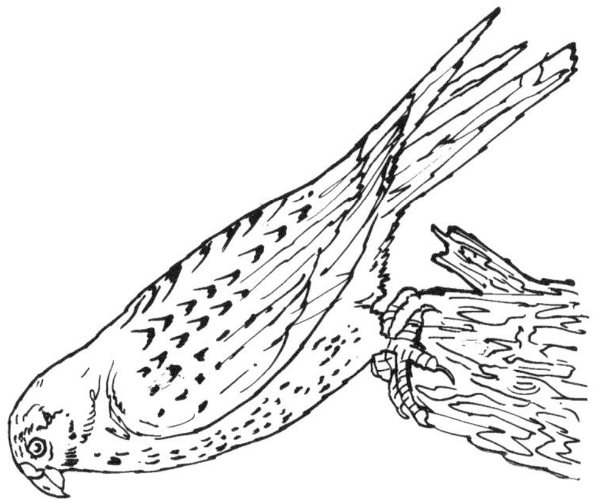

10

12

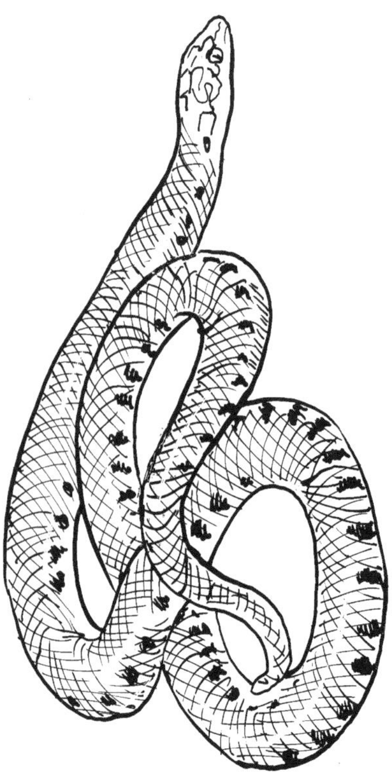

7

9

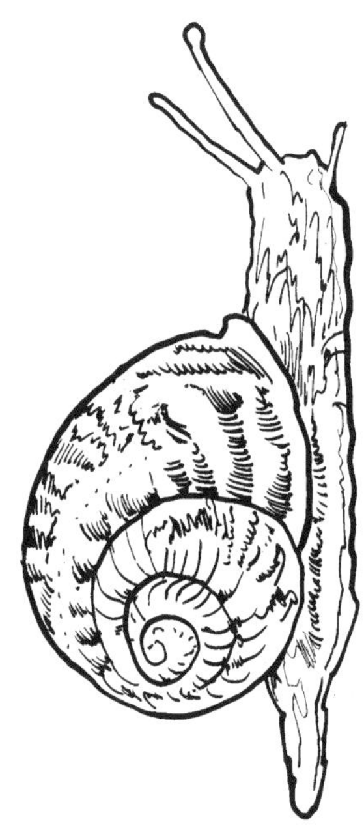

11

esource sheet 11: Where do I Live? 3

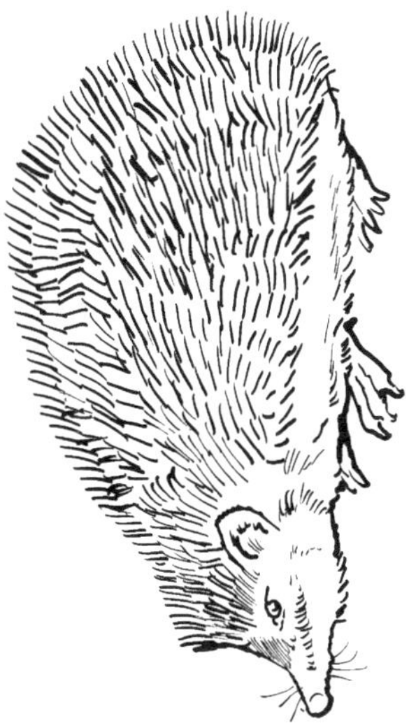

14

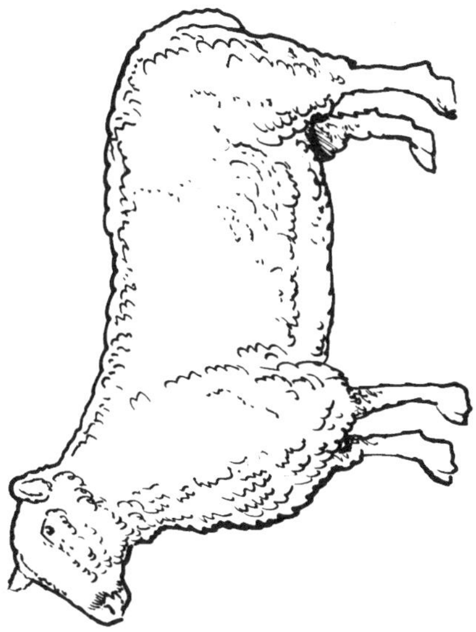

16

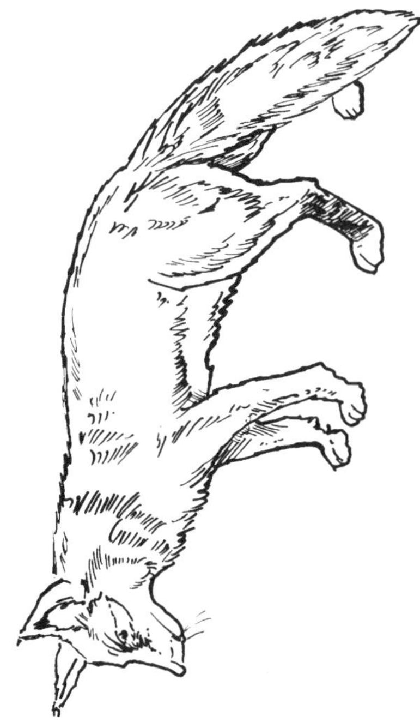

18

13

15

17

Resource sheet 12: Where do I Live? 4

1

2

3

esource sheet 13: Where do I Live? 5

4

5

6

Resource sheet 14: Where do I Live? 6

Resource sheet 16: How Hot are You? 2

A1

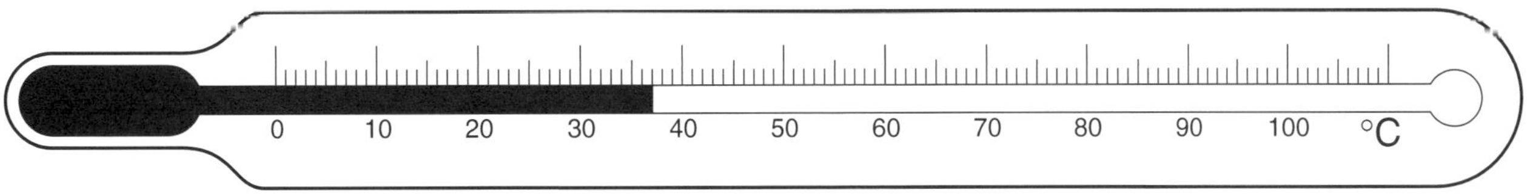

A2

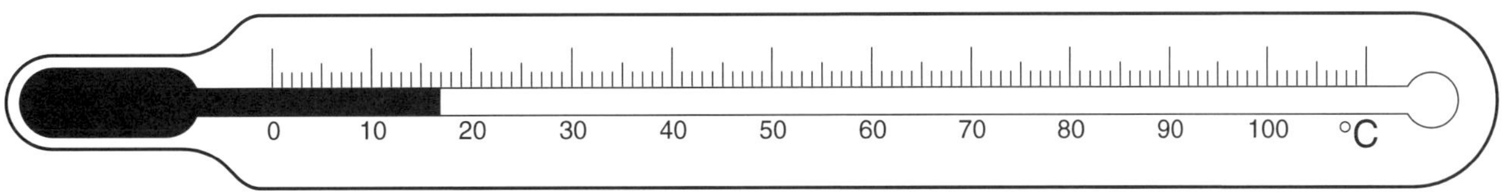

A3

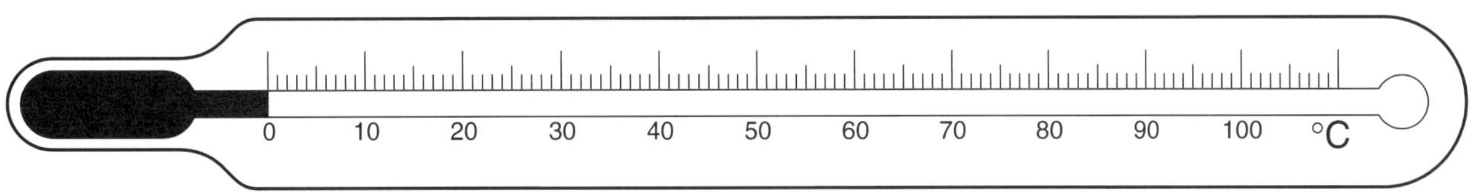

A4

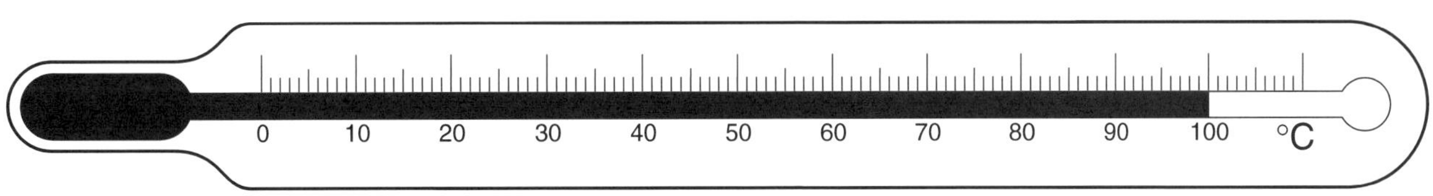

B1

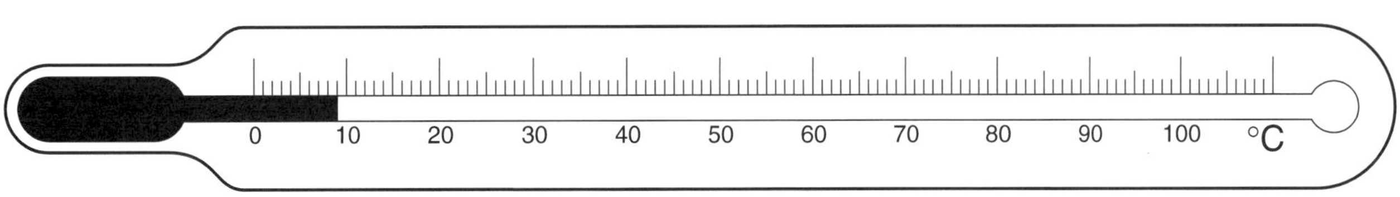

B2

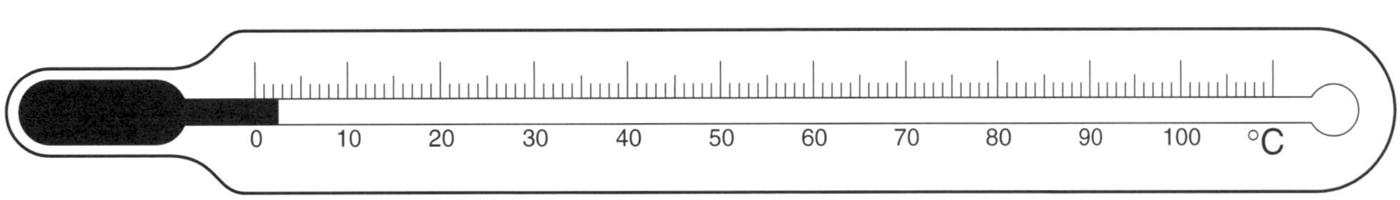

Resource sheet 17: How Hot are You? 3

B3

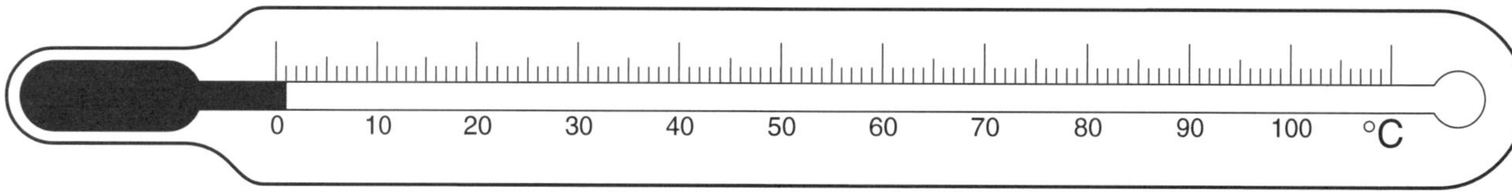

B4

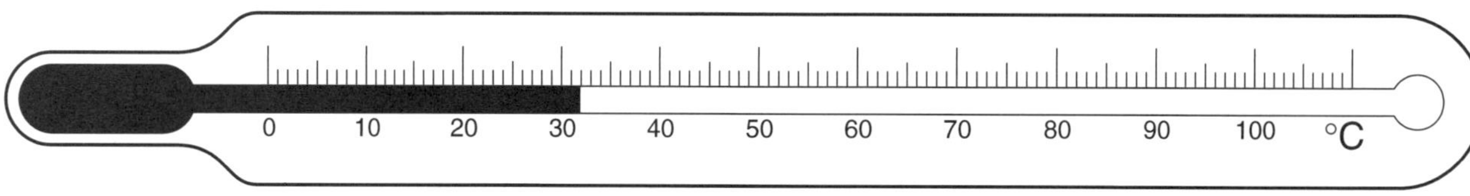

B5

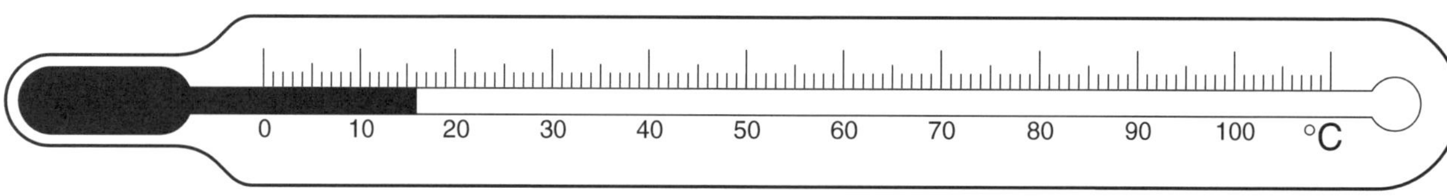

B6

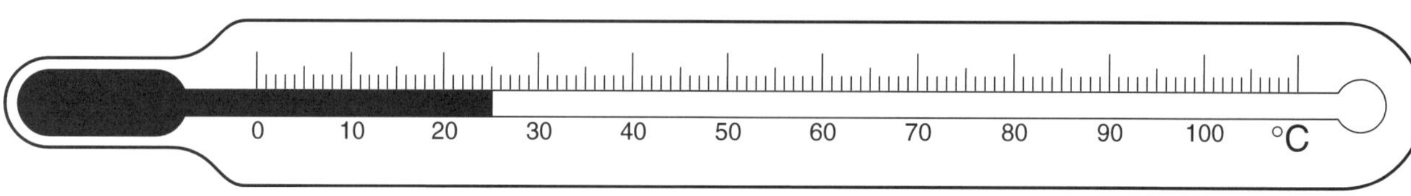

B7

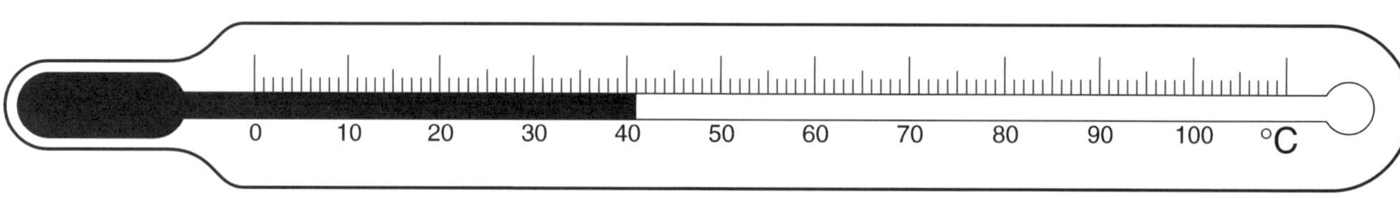

B8

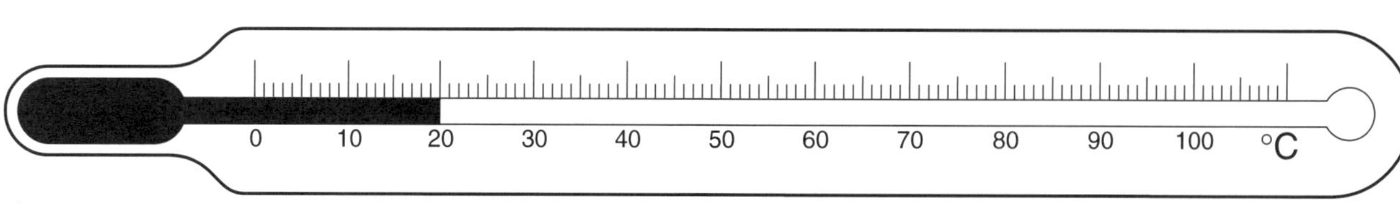

esource sheet 18: How Hot are You? 4

A **a healthy person**	**B** **a person with 'flu**	**B** **a glass of lemonade just poured from a bottle in the fridge**
A **boiling water**	**B** **a glass of water just taken from the tap**	**B** **the classroom at midday in September**
A **an ice cube**	**B** **a garden pond at midday in July**	**B** **the classroom at midday in July**
A **the classroom at midday in December**	**B** **a garden in Spain at midday in August**	**B** **playing in the snow at midday in the winter**

Resource sheet 19: Hotter or Colder?

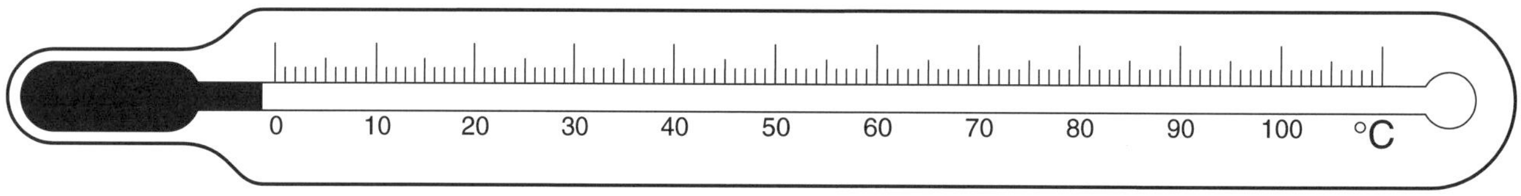

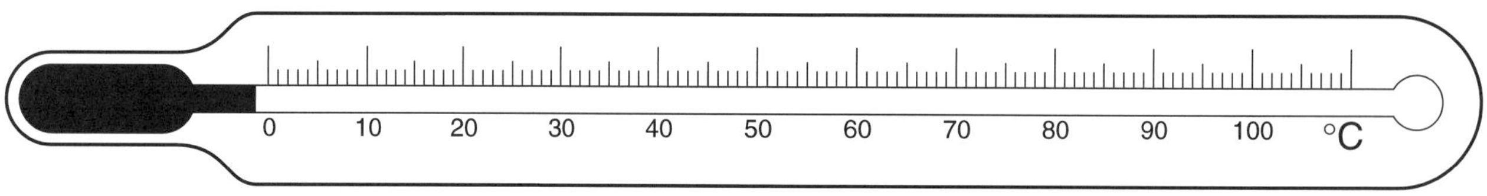

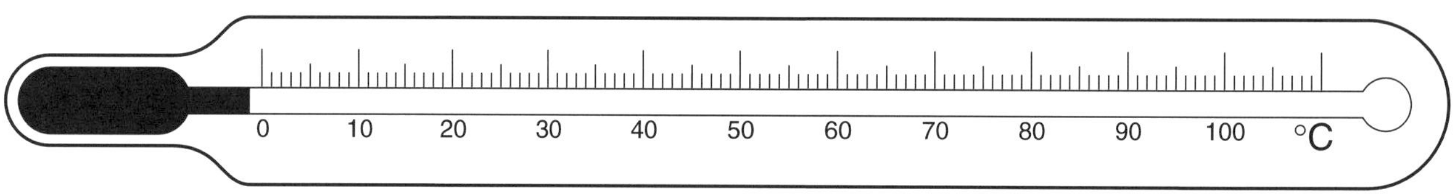

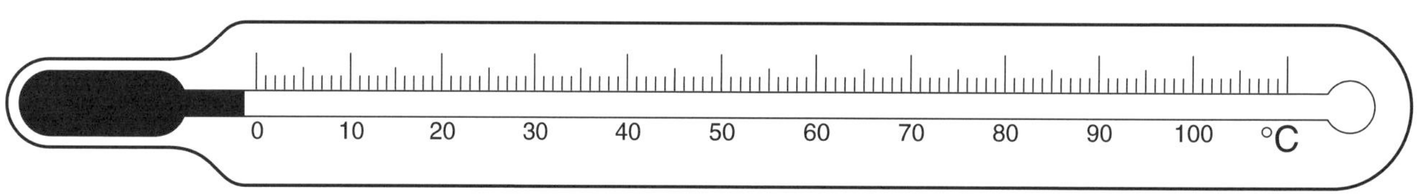

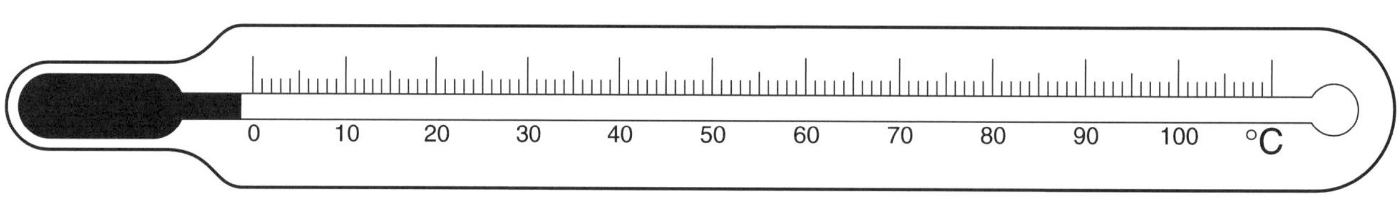

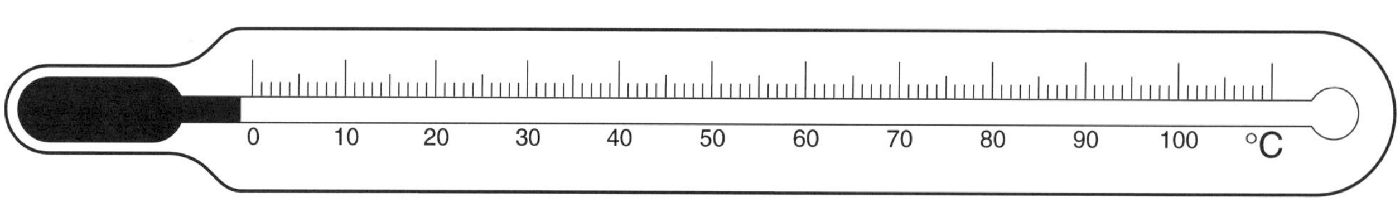

Resource sheet 20: Solids and Liquids 1

shampoo	**lard**
plaster of Paris	**flour**
tea	**cotton wool**
foil	**sugar**
salt	**beads**
bath foam	**orange juice**

Resource sheet 21: Solids and Liquids 2

vinegar	talcum powder
milk	water
a sponge	sand
yoghurt	cooking oil
coffee	rice
tissue	jelly

esource sheet 22: Friction

A1 a person walking	**A2** a book lying on a table
A3 a person swimming	**A4** a car travelling up a hill
B1 a ball bouncing	**B2** a parachutist at 40m above ground
B3 an aeroplane flying	**B4** fruit growing on a tree
B5 a bird perched on a branch	**B6** a bird flying
B7 a person hopping	**B8** a car travelling down a hill

Resource sheet 23: Do I Work?

1

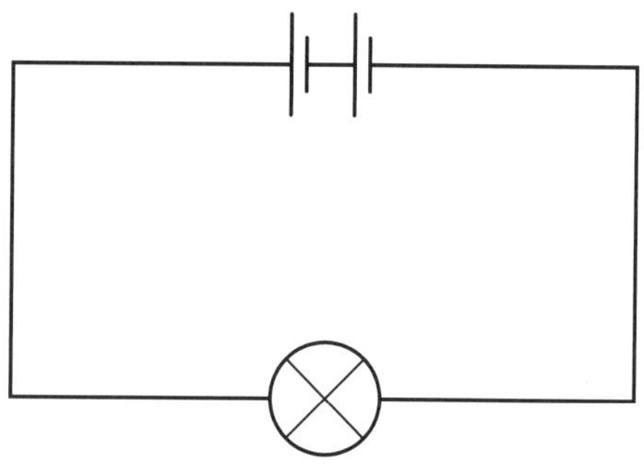

2

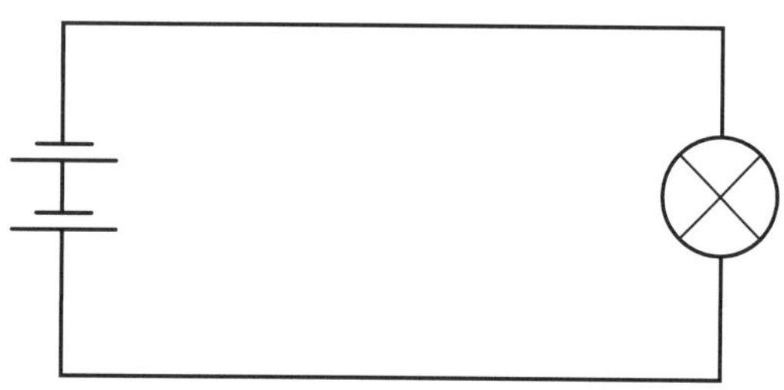

3

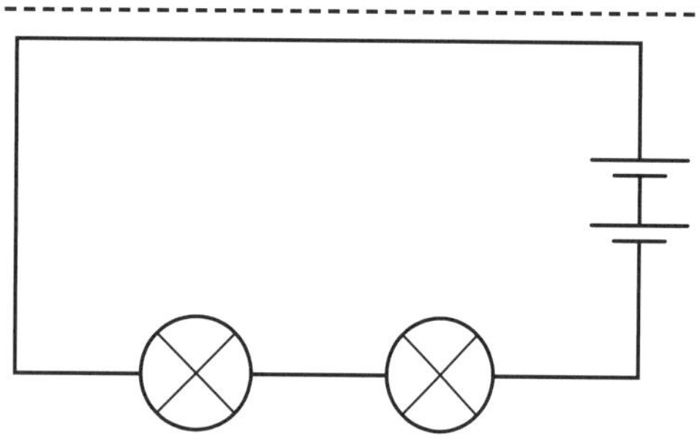

4

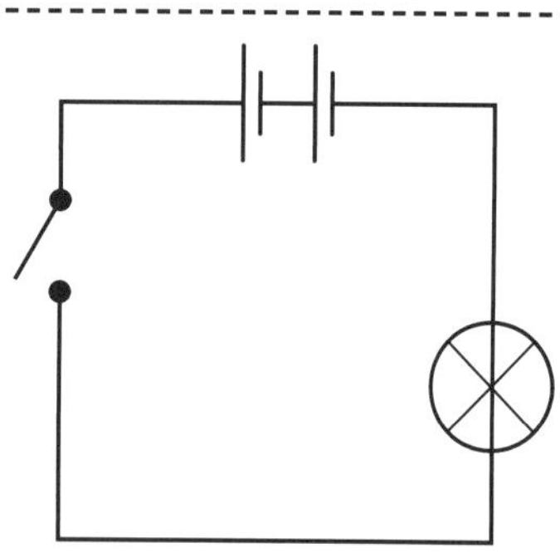

5

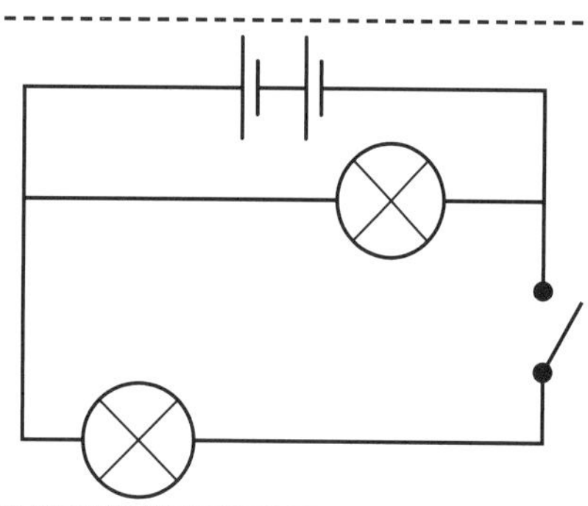

6

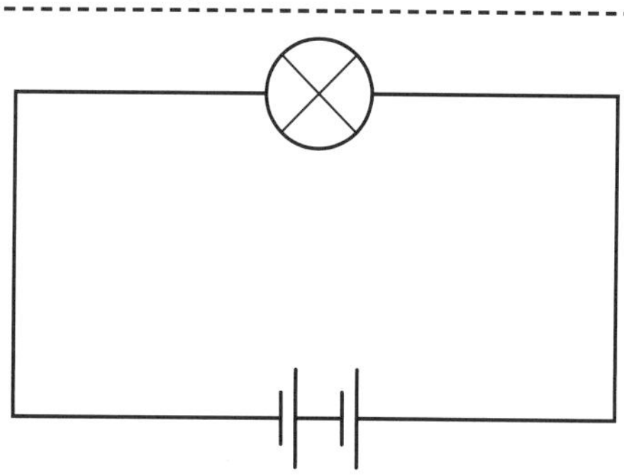

7

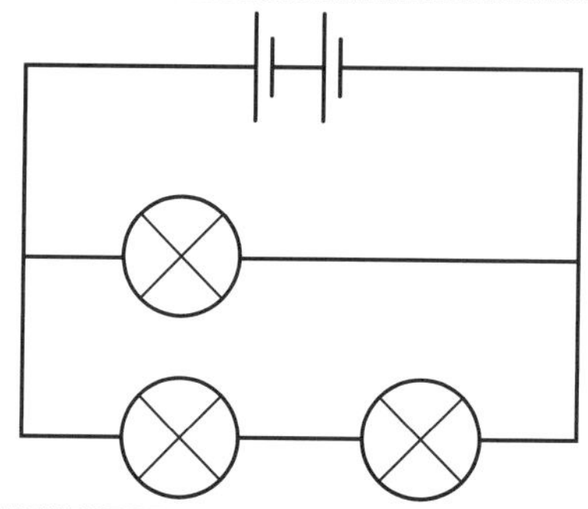

8

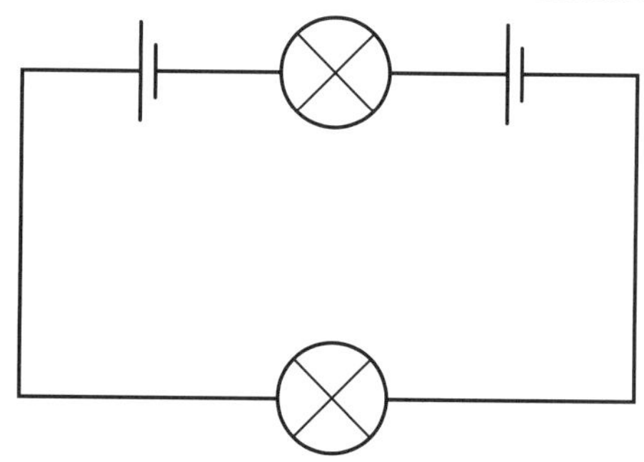

9

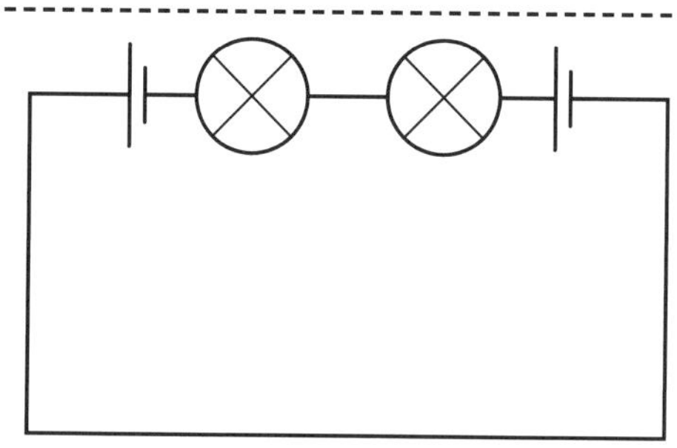

10

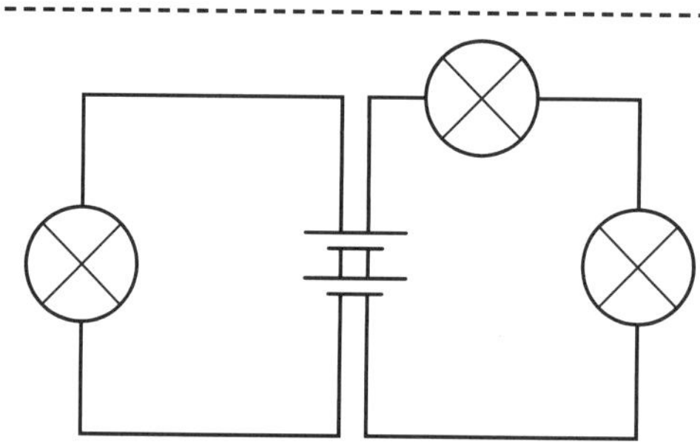

11

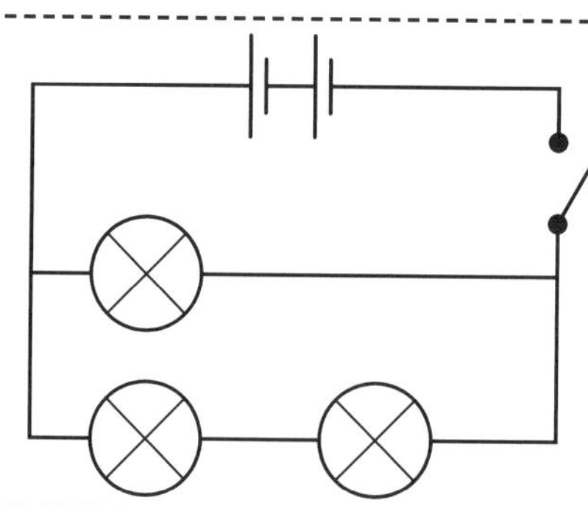

12

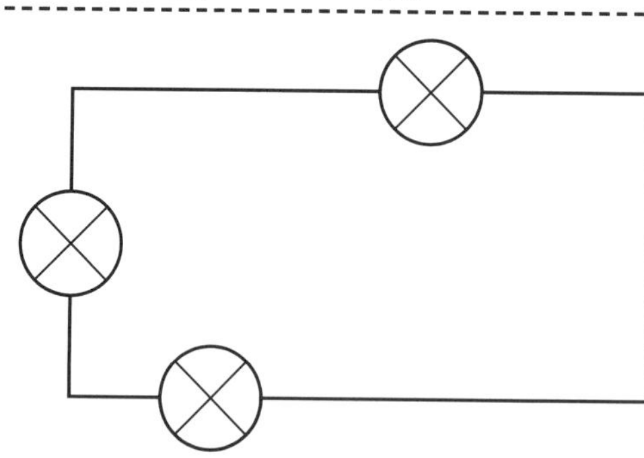

Further Reading

ADEY, P., NAGY, F., ROBERTSON, A., SERRET, N. and WADSWORTH, P. (2003). *Let's Think through Science! Developing thinking with seven- and eight-year-olds.* London: nferNelson.

ADEY, P., ROBERTSON, A. and VENVILLE, G. (2001). *Let's Think! A Programme for developing Thinking in five- and six-year-olds.* London: nferNelson.

ADEY, P., ROBERTSON, A. and VENVILLE, G. (2002). 'Effects of a cognitive acceleration programme on Year 1 pupils.' *British Journal of Educational Psychology*, 72,1,1–25. (A description of the effects of the Let's Think! programme.)

ADEY, P., SHAYER, M. and YATES, C. (2001). *Thinking Science: the Materials of the CASE Project*, 3rd Edition. Cheltenham: Nelson–Thornes. (The published version of the CASE course, for use with older children.)

GOSWAMI, U. (1988). *Cognition in Children.* Hove: Psychology Press. (An excellent account of the development of cognition in young children.)

SHAYER, M. and ADEY, P. (2002). *Learning Intelligence: Cognitive Acceleration Across the Curriculum from 5 to 15 years.* Oxford: Oxford University Press.

SHAYER, M., ADHAMI, M. and ROBERTSON, A. (2004). *Let's Think through Maths!* London: nferNelson.

VYGOTSKY, L. (1978). *Mind in Society: Development of Higher Psychological Processes.* Cambridge, MA: Harvard University Press. (Beautifully translated and well worth dipping into.)

WADSWORTH, B. (1996). *Piaget's Theories of Cognitive and Affective Development: Foundations of Constructivism.* New York: Longman. (A very readable book.)

Notes